GEORGIAN & REGENCY HOUSES EXPLAINED

— TREVOR YORKE —

COUNTRYSIDE BOOKS
NEWBURY BERKSHIRE

First published 2007
© Trevor Yorke 2007
Reprinted 2009, 2016

COUNTRYSIDE BOOKS
3 Catherine Road
Newbury, Berkshire

To view our complete range of books,
please visit us at
www.countrysidebooks.co.uk

ISBN 978 1 84674 051 0

Photographs and illustrations
by the author

All material for the manufacture of this book
was sourced from sustainable forests.

Designed by Peter Davies, Nautilus Design
Produced through The Letterworks Ltd., Reading
Typeset by KT Designs, St Helens
Printed by The Holywell Press, Oxford

CONTENTS

Introduction

Whether it is the grand, symmetrical façades embellished with classical motifs or towering terraces repeated in endless rows or arranged around clumps of greenery, the Georgian and Regency houses conjure up a distinct and much admired image. Elegance, refinement and beautiful proportions have made the classically inspired urban terrace or larger detached house from this period a major influence for later architects and a popular choice for the modern house buyer. They offer a grand aspect with impressively tall rooms and are decorated with restraint, giving them a timeless quality that offends few and attracts many.

Yet what lies behind these idyllic façades? When you strip away the veneer of stone, brick or render, what will you find beneath? The answer is often surprising and very revealing about the period. It is principally with these Georgian and Regency urban terraces and detached houses in mind that this book looks behind the classical public face and explains how they were built, originally laid out and designed, their appearance inside and who owned them. It is intended, too, as an easy to understand guide, illustrated with my own drawings, diagrams and photos, to help give the reader a background knowledge of all aspects of the Georgian and Regency house, whether they are renovating, tracing the history of their own property, or simply interested in this notable period.

The book is divided into three sections. The first describes the development, structure and design of the houses. It begins by outlining the story of the Georgian period, the events that shaped the country, the social changes of the time, urban expansion and the Industrial and Agricultural Revolutions. All these directly influenced the demand, location and type of housing from this period. It then goes further to describe the plans, materials and construction of these new homes before finally looking at the changing fashions of the exterior, with drawings and photos to aid the recognition of the different styles and the date when they were likely to have been built.

The second section goes inside and looks at the different rooms and their fittings, what were they used for and how would they have originally appeared. The third is a quick reference guide with notes on the dating of houses, suggested books to further any research, places to visit and a glossary to explain some of the terms used.

Trevor Yorke

5

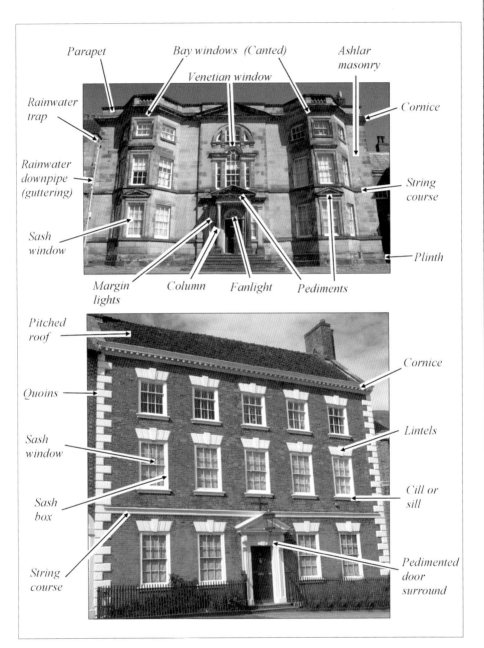

FIG 1.0: *Façades of a stone and brick house with labels of the parts.*

SECTION I

THE HISTORY
OF GEORGIAN AND
REGENCY HOUSES

CHAPTER 1

The Background

FIG 1.1: CHISWICK HOUSE, LONDON: *One of the first great Palladian mansions, built in the 1720s by the 3rd Earl of Burlington, who promoted the architecture of Palladio and Inigo Jones, both influencing the design of 18th century houses. Palladio was arguably the first professional architect, working in 16th century Italy and publishing his theories and designs for later generations to interpret. Inigo Jones brought this classical style to these shores in the early 17th century and created buildings way ahead of his time, ones that were not appreciated and imitated until brought back to life by Burlington and his disciples.*

A Brief History of the Georgian Period

Two principal themes from popular culture and school history textbooks tend to dominate most views of the Georgian period. On one side there is the image of the classical country house set in vast, sweeping parkland, with sensitive gentlemen being whisked away in carriages to formal city squares where walking and dining seemed the main preoccupations. It is a world of elegance, indulgence and wealth dominated by aristocratic families, shaped by Robert Adam and Capability Brown and recorded by Gainsborough.

On the other side there are the Industrial and Agricultural Revolutions, with new townscapes of fiery furnaces, smoking chimneys and back to back housing contrasting with a countryside divided up into regular units, the preserve of the wealthier local families. It is the time of the inventor and entrepreneur, Watt, Trevithick, Wedgwood and Boulton, and of rural revolution in the form of enclosure and emparkment, the move from husbandry to farming for a profit.

The commonly perceived images listed above, however, are only part of the picture, and one which either changed little or slowly at best, and was far from complete by the end of this period. Although this Age of Reason where the medieval and modern worlds met was shaped by a drive for improvement, commercial expansion and the threat of revolution, a powerful aristocracy and ancient institutions still held a tight grip on the reins. Despite the gradual sapping of power to Parliament, the monarchy still sat at the top of the pile, selecting ministers and directing policy, and the succession of each was still a cause for concern, no more so than when Queen Anne, the last of the House of Stuart, died in 1714.

THE HOUSE OF HANOVER

How did the Elector of Hanover (one of the series of small German states, which did not form themselves into the modern-day country until 1870) find himself the king of England in 1714 and the first of the four Georges from which the period is named? The answer lies with the previous Stuart kings who had Catholic sympathies that were wisely kept under wraps in a country in mortal fear of a return to the old faith they had so painfully broken away from in the 16th century. However, when James II came to the throne in 1685 the problem returned to the fore. This arrogant, ill-advised king made no secret of his Roman Catholic conversion and attempted to position men of similar faith in high office. With the birth of his son in 1688 it became clear that a Catholic dynasty threatened and a group, including the Bishop of London, invited William of Orange, the son of one of James's sisters and the husband of James's daughter Mary, to take the throne. His subsequent landing with, in effect, a Dutch invasion force resulted in James, who had lost the support of Parliament and the armed forces, to turn and run, surrendering his throne but not abdicating.

To ensure a Protestant succession the Act of Settlement was passed in 1701, which required any future monarch to be a member of the Church of England. This was a position which Anne, the second daughter of James II, embraced wholeheartedly when she ascended the throne on the death of the childless William in 1702. Her tragedy was that her seventeen children all died in infancy except William who lived to only eleven, so upon her death in 1714 it was feared that the succession would be threatened by the son of James II, the arguably rightful heir to the throne known as the Old Pretender. The 1701 Act had to go back to the children of James I to find a Protestant succession, with the crown being passed on to the grandson of his daughter Elizabeth, who had married a German prince. With the Jacobites (the followers of James Stuart, from *Jacob*, the Latin for his name) disorganised, the new Hanoverian King George took the throne with little opposition, the expected threat from the Old Pretender being defeated in the following year.

George I could barely speak a word of English, preferred to spend his time in his beloved homeland and was surrounded by controversy over the imprisonment of his wife and the suspicious death of her lover, especially when his bones turned up under the floor of one of the king's palaces! His most notable act was leaving the country in the hands of Robert Walpole, whose dominant political position made him in effect our first Prime Minister, and ushered in a period of relative political stability after the turmoil of the previous century.

The king's son, George II, who succeeded him in 1727, was still influenced by his German upbringing and, as with many of his predecessors, was happy to share the court with his wife and a series of mistresses. His other passion was warfare and at the age of 60 he became the last English monarch to fight on the front line, in this case against the old enemy France. The main threat of his reign, however, came from the Young Pretender, Bonnie Prince Charlie, who led a Jacobite invasion in 1745 to reclaim the throne,

FIG 1.2: PICKFORD'S HOUSE, FRIAR GATE, DERBY: *This house, dating from around 1770, was built by Joseph Pickford on the road along which, only 25 years earlier, Bonnie Prince Charlie had ridden into Derby during the rebellion of 1745. This was the furthest south he reached before turning back and being defeated in the following year at Culloden. Today the house is an excellent museum with a totally restored interior and garden.*

reaching as far south as Derby before returning to Scotland. He was defeated by George's brother, the Duke of Cumberland, at Culloden in the following year, which in effect ended the Catholic threat to the throne.

The succession skipped a generation to George II's grandson in 1760, a young man who having been brought up on this isle could claim to be English. Much has been made of George III's bouts of madness but the

FIG 1.3: PARK CRESCENT, LONDON:
Part of the Regents Street and Park development built by John Nash for the Prince Regent, later George IV.

insanity was probably misdiagnosed and exaggerated, in part by his son, the future Prince Regent, who like the other Hanoverian kings was a thorn in the side of his father. Despite this, Farmer George, as this enthusiastic agricultural improver was affectionately known, was popular and a devoted family man, setting new moral standards for the monarchy, which came under increased scrutiny in the wake of the French Revolution which began in 1789.

His son, the Prince Regent from 1811 until his father's death in 1820 and George IV for the following ten years, had no such reputation and despite being a society man and connoisseur of the arts was mocked as overweight, vain, dishonourable and a liar. His passing away in 1830 raised barely a murmur from the public and the period

named after his tenure, the Regency, and its distinctive and colourful architecture credits him with a place in history that his character little deserved. His ill equipped successor, Silly Billy as he was known to the family, never expected to be king and yet in his short seven year reign William IV restored dignity to the throne and played a vital part in the passing through Parliament of the Reform Act of 1832.

POLITICS AND WAR
Reform of Parliament was well overdue by this time as the electoral system was still medieval with patterns of representation that protected aristocratic rule but hardly matched the new urban populations that had developed through the Georgian period. Despite this lack of change there were many aspects that had improved as it grew in influence and power throughout the 18th century. Rather than being called upon only when the monarch required funds, Parliament now sat at a regular time each year, the arrival in London of the MPs and their entourage (generally in autumn) signalling the start of the 'Season'. This lasted through to the following spring, a social whirlwind that in turn affected the development of the capital. Stability had also been achieved with a seven year length of government rather than the previous three year term. Other important changes were the appearance of salaried civil servants who were awarded positions on merit rather than by connections, and the development of long-term planning, commissions and

white papers, with political parties formed around policies rather than patronage.

The Georgian kings and their governments generally believed in a non-interference policy, removing restrictions for economic expansion and giving a free rein to companies, private individuals and financial institutions. However, they operated by different rules when it came to warfare! Spurred on by trading interests and a dislike, especially, of the French, Britain became interwoven in European politics and fought what were openly termed as 'commercial wars' with the reward of territorial gains and the resulting increase in trade the carrot dangling at the end of the stick. The country was generally successful in this policy, finding itself by the end of the period with a massive empire bound together by trade and protected by the Royal Navy, which ensured supplies of raw materials and foods and a ready market for its manufactured goods in return.

However, the loss of the colonies in 1783 after defeat in the American War of Independence and the threat of invasion from France during 1793 to 1815 caused disruption in the economy and society back home, with those on the bottom rung of the ladder usually suffering worst. The after effects of this latter conflict posed the greatest threat to the authorities, with post war economic depression, hundreds of thousands of disbanded soldiers looking for work, poor harvests, protest rallies and the threat of revolution. The Reform Act of 1832 was in part a reaction to quell this by granting the vote to a wider proportion of the middle classes, although any ideas of democracy and working class representation were far from their thoughts.

AGRICULTURE, INDUSTRY AND TRANSPORT

Despite increased trade and commercial growth, agriculture remained the dominant industry and cornerstone of the economy throughout most of this period. The wealthy relied upon rents from tenants on their estates and they in turn upon a healthy market for their produce, which increasingly went for sale rather than sustenance. The variable demand, warfare and the weather created a fluctuating picture but after poor years in the 1730s and 40s agriculture generally picked up, especially in areas where new enclosures had reorganised the fields into more efficient units.

Industry at this stage was widespread but generally small in scale and even where large works or mills were constructed much of the manufacturing process was carried out by families at home in the surrounding town and villages. As with agriculture, the drive for improvement was a defining character of the age. Financially supported by wealthy family members or others from the same religious group, inventors and entrepreneurs from even modest backgrounds could now design, conduct experiments and market their products on a larger scale.

There were two key factors in the growth of industry, the first being the

FIG 1.4: MASSON MILLS, CROMFORD, DERBYSHIRE: *The second mill built by Richard Arkwright at Cromford, dating from 1783. Although the cotton was spun in this water-powered mill, other processes were carried out in houses, many built by Arkwright, in the neighbouring village (see Fig 2.15).*

from deeper workings. The second factor was the improvement of the river navigations and development of a canal network, which reached a peak of construction in the 1790s. Transporting raw materials to site and the finished product away had restricted industrial growth as roads were too poor for heavy goods to be moved any distance and rivers were affected by droughts, flooding and obstructions, principally from mills. The canals were engineered to solve many of these seasonal problems and to reach areas not served by rivers, with the effect that the price of goods was reduced and new factories and settlements sprang up along their banks.

Passenger travel witnessed equally dramatic improvements. The thought of going from one part of the country to another in previous centuries either was not required by a generally insular population or dreaded by the few that had to. The journey was rough, unreliable and fraught with danger, most famously from highwaymen, and services that might run only once a week from London to the provinces could take days to reach their destination rather than the hours they would take today. Improved communication was another key element in the growth of industry and spread of ideas and it came with the breeding of stronger and fitter horses, more organised and regular services and the creation of turnpike trusts. Since Tudor times local parishes had been responsible for the generally poor maintenance of roads, but from the early 18th century turnpike trusts (named after the rising gate or 'turn pike' where tolls had to be

steam engine. A restriction upon the early industrial workings of the 16th and 17th centuries was power which, as it principally came from waterwheels, limited the location and was susceptible to seasonal fluctuations in supply. The development of an efficient steam engine by Thomas Newcomen and its further improvement by James Watt gave a more flexible and reliable source of power and crucially carried out the pumping of water from mines so that the raw materials of industry could be extracted

FIG 1.5: *Mileposts were erected by turnpike trusts along the length of road for which they were responsible.*

paid) took over lengths of roads with the intention of improving the surface for a fee. This was done to such an extent that by the second half of the

FIG 1.6: CROMFORD WHARF, DERBYSHIRE: *The terminus of the Cromford Canal, built for a consortium including Richard Arkwright whose earlier mill stands opposite, and opened in 1793 at the height of Canal Mania.*

century more than 15,000 miles had been taken over. However, the standard did not always improve and the tolls charged were resented, especially as the rich got away without paying, so that the hated gates and their keepers were often targets for rioters.

Georgian Society

After years of stagnation the population of the country began to grow in the second half of the 18th century, for reasons that are still not clear, although access to better food and housing – and soap – may have all played their part. Outbreaks of disease were still rife, particularly in the mid century, and the resilient population that emerged afterwards saw growth from around six million up to nine million by the turn of the 19th century. Much of this expansion came from London alone, which nearly tripled in numbers in this period to more than one and a half million by 1830. Other towns and cities were tiny in comparison but growth was even more dramatic in industrial centres and ports. For instance, Manchester, a modest town with under 10,000 people at the beginning of this period, had swelled to a potential city of 180,000 by the end of it.

Despite these growing concentrations of population, the majority still lived in the country and worked on the land, even in the midst of the Industrial Revolution. The social mix also only changed slowly in this period, with the bulk of the nation's wealth in the hands of aristocratic and gentry families, which probably made up just a few percent of the population, and under-

FIG 1.7: *This magnificent room at Kedleston Hall, Derbyshire was designed by Robert Adam in the 1770s. It displays the aristocracy's love for Ancient Greece and Rome, inspired by their Grand Tours and the work of Palladio, and turned into reality by leading architects of the day.*

pinned by a growing yet still small middle class. More than three-quarters of the people in England were crafts-men, labourers, or vagrants with no representation, few rights, and a life potentially full of violent fluctuations in fortune. Surprisingly, though, rich and poor lived side by side in many areas, and it was common for a large house of a wealthy family in town to have narrow courts of working class dwellings at the rear, although the exodus to peace and privacy in the suburbs for those with money had already begun.

UPPER CLASSES

For the hereditary aristocratic families and the wealthiest gentlemen, the Georgian period was generally one where their incomes grew as land, the ownership of which was still the main status symbol in society, increased in value. This could happen due to suburban development, agricultural improvement or through the extraction of minerals and if it did not, as was often the case early on in the period, they could marry a rich heiress!

There were, however, an increasing number of delights and opportunities on which they could spend their money, and some still managed to get into debt. For many a young gentleman the climax of his education would have been the Grand Tour, a journey primarily to Italy to soak up the archi-tectural and cultural wonders of the Classical Age and invariably buy up and cart half of it back with him! Second sons were increasingly attracted to the church, which, as the land attached to each living gained value, became a lucrative position. However, as they mixed in a different social circle they often became rather remote in their smart new vicarage from their parishioners, weakening the Church's influence on their minds and souls.

The main expense for this class was building a country house. A need for increased space, often to store all the artwork and sculpture shipped back from the Continent, and the demands of socialising were usually enough motivation. There was also the desire to impress guests with their refined taste for classical style but with the most modern of fittings behind the antique appearance. This resulted in large-scale rebuilding of thousands of country houses (most were refaced or extended; fewer were built completely from scratch due to the huge costs involved). The estate that it commanded came under the same scrutiny as landscapes were altered to mirror those of the classical world. They also provided a base for the new sports of foxhunting and shooting, in the process sweeping communities aside and breaking the traditional bond between manor house and manor.

Much of the year was spent in London or in the major provincial town or city where the aristocratic and gentry families would either own or rent a large house, attracted by business or parliamentary commitments and the social circle and leisure opportunities on offer. For those who could afford it there were assembly rooms for concerts, dances and gatherings, theatres for plays, and coffee and chocolate houses for meetings (which developed into Gentlemen's Clubs later in the period). There were many other distractions, mistresses were common and illegitimate children numerous, gambling was the downfall of many a gentleman and drinking a serious problem (this is the time when the phrase 'drunk as a lord' was coined). It was not until later in the period that those in power developed a more dignified and sober image under the threat of revolution from below.

Crime and rioting were two other problems that faced the rich, especially as there was no police force, and both were accepted as part of life. Their houses were natural targets for burglars and rioters and they attempted to protect them with external shutters and elaborate door locks, which still survive on some properties today. Petty crime

FIG 1.8: *Shutters were commonly fitted to ground floor windows of upper and middle class houses, not only to protect delicate interiors from excessive sunlight but also, when the property was unoccupied, to deter thieves and rioters. The bolt was fastened from inside when they were shut, with a rotating stay (between the two shutters) holding them in place (see also Fig 4.34).*

was rife in places and it was even known for wigs to be snatched off the heads of the unwary in the middle of the street! The only answer the authorities could come up with was to lower the offence by which you could be hung or transported – pickpocketing as little as 12 pence could send you to the gallows – although it appears that this action was no deterrent.

MIDDLE CLASSES

Below the wealthiest band of society were increasing numbers of professionals, businessmen, merchants, financiers, shopkeepers and farmers whose rising income permitted them to imitate their superiors' lifestyle. In the first half of the period they tended to be subservient to the gentry but by the turn of the 19th century they began to form the distinctive characteristics we associate with middle class life, becoming critical of upper class behaviour, establishing groups promoting the Church and Sunday schools and campaigning against vice and slavery. Many of them began the 18th century working in 'trades' but by the end were described as 'professionals'. One example were architects who were formerly gentlemen amateurs (Vanbrugh who designed Blenheim Palace began his career in the army) but by the early 19th century were trained experts with their own practices. The middle classes were, however, at this time still only a small proportion of the population with the largest concentration, probably around one in five, being in the capital. This expanding social group was one of the main driving forces for the building of the new terraced houses that will be the main subject of this book.

LOWER CLASSES

The vast majority of the population came under this broad banner, which could include a skilled craftsman in a brick-built cottage or terrace down to a casual labourer in a mud hovel, and below this an underclass of homeless vagrants. Compared with today, life in the town or city could mean unbearably long hours of work, irregular incomes, limited freedom and short life expectancy. Disease was rife,

sanitation virtually non-existent, food was poor with most income going on bread, and wages often kept low in the belief that this would make workers more industrious.

This drudgery started at an early age, with many of the poorest or orphaned children put to work as young as five. Some of the worst conditions were inflicted upon chimney sweeps' climbing boys who were starved to make them thin enough, although many still got stuck and if they did not die from this treatment they often developed cancer of the scrotum. In the country, things were little better and living conditions often worse, with daily life heavily affected by harvests, local disasters and changing weather. Those with the smallest holdings tended to lose out, especially if the village was subject to emparkment or parliamentary enclosure.

Compared with previous generations, however, the under classes at this time may have looked more favourably upon their lot. The increased wealth of the nation filtered down to this level with better wages or cheaper goods for some, although pay was irregular, varied dramatically between regions and trades and there was little security if employment dried up. Those coming into industrial centres from the country often found the rigid hours and regular wages of factory work a shock compared with the casual routine of agriculture, and many preferred to work fewer hours rather than labour for more money if times were good.

Most of the family would work, some in domestic service (the largest source of employment outside agriculture) or in mills, mines and factories or producing piecework at home. So, although many families would live in no more than a large single room, the whole family would only occupy it together for a short time each day. It was common for the man of the house to eat and drink out after work; the intake of beer increased and gin consumption boomed in the 1720s and 30s. Public houses were centres of the community, offering entertainment, bull baiting and cock fighting, and they were also places where business could be conducted. For those unable to work the poor law was provided but was only granted within the home parish, so many were reluctant to leave their town or village or had to return to it if work dried up elsewhere. This system, however, designed some two centuries before, could not cope with the new, rapidly expanding urban areas.

The lot of the working classes depended very much on where they lived, especially if this was in one of the urban or rural areas where change occurred. Before looking at the houses built, it is important to examine the new types of town, village and suburb where much of the new housing was erected.

FIG 1.9: STOWE LANDSCAPE GARDENS, BUCKINGHAMSHIRE: *The aristocracy sought to recreate classical views from Ancient Rome in their sweeping landscape gardens and built follies in a variety of styles as eye-catching pieces within the composition. However, in the process, many villages were re-sited or removed completely. Stowe is probably the best example open to the public of this effect. It not only displays outstanding monumental buildings but also retains its original medieval church, hidden behind trees from the original community.*

CHAPTER 2

Georgian and Regency Housing

FIG 2.1: BRIGHTON, SUSSEX: *This street, dating from the 1820s, was one of many built in this booming seaside resort to house the wealthy who had discovered the medicinal properties of sea water and the social delights of the Season. The houses have typical Regency features like the stucco-covered exterior, balconies with decorative iron railings and bay windows through which to glimpse the sea in the far distance.*

A Brief History of Housing

Before the 18th century the vast majority of the population lived in villages and hamlets, working the land or in small-scale industrial activities, with the then small towns and cities serving primarily as markets and administration centres. London was the only major concentration of population and was split between twin centres – finance and trade in the City area and the court further west around Westminster. There were many settlements that grew up around specialist trades like ports, coal mining, and the wool industry, for instance, but these tended to be small in scale, scattered and not always permanent. In the Georgian period new developments in foreign trade, industry, agriculture and leisure resulted in the founding and growth of new towns and villages, forming the basis of the modern distribution of population with which we are familiar.

Urban Development

LONDON

The capital already had ten times the population of the next largest city in England when George I came to the throne and it maintained this dominance, with more than one and a half million residents by the time George IV died. This tripling of numbers during the 115 years of this period came about through a massive influx of people from home and abroad.

Some were escaping persecution in foreign countries and brought with them new skills and trades, others came for jobs in new industries and the docks. The annual sitting of Parliament and the development of the Season encouraged the rich to seek permanent residences in London and with them came a huge infrastructure of domestic servants, coachmen and shop workers to satisfy their every whim. The growth of government and law attracted civil servants and solicitors to the city and other skilled professionals like doctors

FIG 2.2: SPITALFIELDS, LONDON: *French Protestants, nicknamed Huguenots, were one of the largest groups of immigrants in London as they fled persecution back home after Louis XIV revoked the edict that granted them protection in 1685. A large group of them were skilled silk weavers but they had to settle in the Spitalfields area outside the walls of the City of London, which was still controlled by the guilds and merchants. They built many fine early Georgian terraced houses with characteristic long attic windows to cast light on their detailed work.*

and architects to this centre of activity.

Although there were large developments in other parts of the city, the most notable of the new housing built to accommodate this influx took place to the north and west. Here on what

FIG 2.3: SIR JOHN SOANE'S
MUSEUM, 13 LINCOLN'S INN
FIELDS, LONDON: *As with most
leading architects by the turn of the
19th century, Sir John Soane was a
professional who had trained in an
architectural practice and was based in
the capital. His own house, pictured
here, displays his stylised classical
detailing, work that was well ahead
of his time.*

decline in the principal trade. Some saw
rapid expansion, others stagnation and
little building as they became bypassed
by the new industries and business.
One area where there was widespread
rebuilding or re-facing of buildings was
on the main roads in and out of town,
along which the new coaches ran. The
improvement in road surfaces and the
coaches themselves saw a boom in the
servicing of travellers, with inns and
public houses built in new fashionable
styles to attract business. As many
could not afford such costs it was
common for a new brick or rendered
façade to be added to an existing
building to keep up to date, with the
arrangement of openings or exposed

FIG 2.4: HIGH STREET, ST
MARTINS, STAMFORD,
LINCOLNSHIRE: *The Old Great North
Road was an important and busy route
in the 18th century and along this
southern approach into town were
established coaching inns and fine stone
houses. Stamford is still today one of the
most remarkable stone-built towns in the
country and is dominated by medieval
churches and Georgian houses.*

were just fields owned by enterprising
gentry were laid out streets and squares
of refined terraced housing,
speculations designed to attract those
from the polluted, filthy and noisy old
city and newcomers from the country
into fashionable, elegant surroundings.
Ribbons of new housing also spread
out along the coaching routes radiating
out of the city.

PROVINCIAL TOWNS AND
CITIES
The amount of new housing in towns
and cities reflected the growth or

FIG 2.5: THE GEORGE INN, WEST WYCOMBE, BUCKINGHAMSHIRE: *For those who could not afford to rebuild a house or inn, it was very common to have it re-fronted to remain fashionable. This example along the old London to Oxford road has a classical brick façade (above) but from behind its older timber-framed structure is revealed (below). Windows not lining up or sagging horizontally and a front that is not arranged symmetrically are often a clue to an older timber structure behind.*

FIG 2.6: THE CIRCUS, BATH: *Bath was one of the most fashionable centres outside London, with a growing appreciation of the medicinal powers of its spa water. John Wood the Elder and his son John Wood the Younger designed some of the most notable buildings of the time, including The Circus with its pairs of stacked columns inspired by the Colosseum in Rome.*

timber beams within usually betraying the earlier structure behind.

SPA TOWNS AND SEASIDE RESORTS

This improvement in passenger travel opened up new leisure opportunities in far-flung corners of the country that had previously only been appreciated by a limited local clientèle. Rheumatism and skin disorders were just two of the

FIG 2.7: CHELTENHAM, GLOUCESTERSHIRE: *This spa town developed after a visit from King George III and retains much of its Regency housing, as with these large semi-detached houses with characteristic iron balconies.*

FIG 2.9: REGENCY SQUARE, BRIGHTON: *It was the belief that sea water could cure or relieve ailments, either by bathing in it or drinking it, which drew crowds to the south coast and encouraged the building of streets and squares along the sea front, as with this example from the 1820s.*

FIG 2.8: THE CRESCENT, BUXTON, DERBYSHIRE: *Remote locations were not a restriction to Georgians as Buxton, high up in the Peak District, became a fashionable destination for those seeking its natural mineral waters. This building dating from the 1780s was designed by John Carr of York.*

ailments for which the Georgians sought a cure. The drinking of certain mineral waters was one answer, which resulted in a massive expansion of spa towns, firstly and most notably at Bath and later, as they grew in popularity, at Cheltenham, Leamington and Buxton.

The benefits of bathing in sea water were also appreciated in the Regency period and small seaside resorts developed around the country, but no more so than at Brighton where elegant rendered terraces were built along streets and around squares fronting the sea.

PORTS, NAVY DOCKS AND ARMY BARRACKS

The increase in trade with Europe and especially the new colonies resulted in the development and expansion of ports. Liverpool, Whitehaven and Bristol all grew, with new docks and fashionable housing for those who had made their fortune from shipping. The Port of London also expanded, although only after the Thames had become so clogged with traffic that merchants threatened to move elsewhere. Smaller ports developed along rivers where improvements to navigation brought larger craft further inland to dock. The building of new ships

for the merchant fleet led to development in towns like Sunderland and Scarborough and for the navy, which had to protect their routes, in centres at Portsmouth, Chatham and Plymouth.

A permanent standing army took shape in the 18th century, although it was much smaller than the navy. It was principally employed overseas until, with the threat of revolution in the air in the 1790s, new barracks were built to house a force to quell public dissent – this role was, however, largely taken over by the police force in the following century. Army buildings, accommodation and officers' houses were built in many towns and cities, and factories and metal foundries that supplied

FIG 2.10: LIVERPOOL: *This important port grew in the 18th century as a result of trade from the American colonies, Asia and Ireland. Merchants and those involved with shipping built themselves classically styled terraces on the hill overlooking the docks.*

FIG 2.11: STOURPORT BASIN, WORCESTERSHIRE: *Towns also developed further inland around wharfs and docks as with this example on the River Severn, which became a busy canal junction. A new town was laid out with the houses on the far side of the basin built along a rigid grid pattern of straight roads, as is still evident today.*

FIG 2.12: WEEDON BARRACKS, NORTHAMPTONSHIRE: *Permanent barracks only began to be established with the threat from Napoleon and from radicals. This site was principally a depot for light arms but as it was at the geographic centre of England, pavilions were built to house the king in case of invasion. The lodge in the picture incorporated a portcullis (in the arch at the bottom) to cut off the canal, which ran into the site.*

FIG 2.13: CROMFORD, DERBYSHIRE: *This row of terraced houses was built by Richard Arkwright in the 1780s and had living accommodation on the ground and first floors, and an open attic above for weaving with distinctive wide windows.*

weapons for both army and navy also resulted in urban expansion, especially in the Birmingham area.

INDUSTRIAL TOWNS

The most notable urban growth, however, occurred in the new industrial centres in the Midlands and North as towns and cities were established or expanded many times over. The cotton industry in the Manchester area, clothing in Leeds and Halifax and metal working in Sheffield and the West Midlands were some of the more important examples. Smaller settlements also developed in rural areas around mining, iron production and quarrying, many expanding in scattered, unplanned forms where there was little control over the landlord, and only later, with infilling, becoming a more defined town or city.

Rural Development

Despite the expansion of urban areas in this period, the complete transformation of rural communities at the same time could be far more dramatic and thorough. Many remote hamlets remained untouched in this age before railways and mass tourism and others that had been enclosed by agreement in previous centuries may have changed very little. But for vast swathes of the country, especially in the Midlands, the reform of agriculture, the reshaping of country houses, the spread of industry and the expanding transport network caused, in the worst examples, the complete removal of ancient communities.

TURNPIKE AND CANAL SETTLEMENTS

Many smaller settlements also benefited from the increased traffic on the main roads upon which they stood. Others may have been bypassed by new lengths of road constructed by the Turnpike Trust to shorten routes or avoid notorious obstacles or hills but, to avoid missing out on the lucrative trade, inns and buildings were established on the new stretch and a general drift of building away from the old centre to the new source of business often occurred.

With the arrival of canals in the late 18th century, workshops, wharfs, pubs and inns were built to maintain the structure and service the route and its workers. Houses were sited around these new centres, either in existing settlements or a short distance away, with building spreading down towards the activity around the canal.

PARLIAMENTARY ENCLOSURES

In this age of agricultural improvement the medieval arrangement of small-scale farms with scattered holdings in different fields was restrictive to new

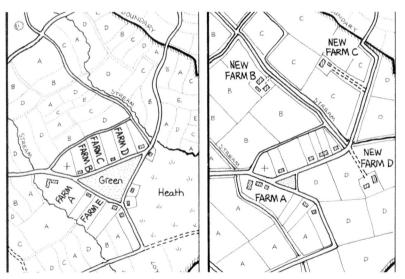

FIG 2.14: *Maps of a simplified imaginary estate and its village around the green before (left) and after (right) Parliamentary enclosure. In the left-hand example the five farmers (A–E) have their houses in the centre of the settlement as their land is dispersed in the large fields around. In the right-hand map, however, new farmhouses have been built out in their newly rearranged holdings, but farmer E has lost his land to his larger neighbours.*

FIG 2.15: EDENSOR, DERBYSHIRE: *This village was re-sited in the 1830s to keep it out of view of Chatsworth House. The new buildings were designed in an eclectic mix of styles more for the pleasure of the lord than his tenants.*

ideas and practices. Some areas had already been enclosed (the process of hedging or fencing off the land of individuals) by agreement. However, landlords of estates where this had not been possible now looked to friends in Parliament to pass acts forcing it upon their tenants. This reached a peak of activity in the late 18th and early 19th century, with previously large open fields and common land being divided up into regular sized compartments and new straight roads with wide verges (often mistaken for Roman roads) constructed between them.

This created more manageable and efficient farms that could meet the new urban demand for food. The tenants with the greatest amount of land could build new brick and stone farmhouses located in the centre of their holdings (their old houses back in the village were often subdivided up for cottages), which could be held on simplified leases of 7 to 21 years. Smallholders, however, often lost out, not only losing their land but also the common rights to graze livestock on village greens and wasteland, which were swallowed up in the reorganisation. A large part of the rural population became seasonal labourers or moved to the new industrial centres.

EMPARKMENT AND ESTATE VILLAGES

The relationship between the lord of the manor and his tenants had gradually changed over the centuries. The old manor house with its open door to villagers and visitors alike had become more remote, with firstly tall walls around it and then removal to a more private corner. In the 18th century many landowners sought to transform their piece of rural England into a romantic classical scene and the scattered hovels they could view from the house did not fit in. Rather than re-site their home, many preferred to remove the entire village to a completely new position out of sight. The process of emparkment often started with the enclosure of the estate, then new houses for the villagers were built, before the old buildings (many of which may have been simple timber framed cottages of limited life) were flattened. The old church was often the only building left standing close to the

FIG 2.16: NUNEHAM COURTENAY, OXFORDSHIRE: *These cottages date from the 1760s when the village was re-sited along the new turnpike road, a mile from its old position next to the grand country house. Only the church remained and it was given a classical makeover to fit in with the new building.*

country house, perhaps with a fashionable classical makeover, so it was only a short walk for the lord of the manor on a Sunday. On paper this may seem to have benefited both parties, but as part of the reorganisation many landlords took the opportunity to remove unwanted villagers by only offering the new houses to the best tenants, and then on strict terms.

Other estate villages that remained in place or had a partial removal were often rebuilt by wealthy landlords, less

out of benevolence to their tenants and more to improve the approach to their own house to impress guests! (At Old Warden in Bedfordshire the tenants themselves had to dress up in period costume to complete the landlord's picturesque view of the world.)

Types of Development

LANDLORDS AND BUILDERS

In the past, houses were generally erected for the tenant or landowner by a builder or by the owner himself. There were planned developments at least as far back as the 12th century and most towns and even villages have elements that may have originated thus, but nothing on the scale or with the permanency that emerged in London in the mid 17th century. These first speculative projects were laid out upon what were then open fields, with straight rows of new brick terraced housing.

Some of these new permanent structures were built by an emerging breed of small-scale speculators, often but not always builders. They would take the risk of building the house and having to find a purchaser or tenant for it afterwards in return for a low ground rent and a long-term lease, around 30–40 years. When the lease ran out, the buildings would revert back to the original landlord who could then increase the rent. These original terms meant that there was little incentive to build houses that would last longer than the length of the lease and poor quality construction was often the result. In response, the terms were increased so that by the mid 18th

FIG 2.17: THE CRESCENT, BATH: *This most famous of buildings in Bath was designed by John Wood the Younger in the 1770s. However, he commissioned a series of different builders to construct it and although they had to stick rigidly to his plan of the façade there are slight differences, as in the close up where the windows are not the same height.*

century 99 years was becoming the norm.

The landlord would usually retain some control over the appearance of the street or estate and larger builders would often design the buildings and then subcontract the work out. Whatever the arrangement, it was common for only a small number of houses to be built at once by one builder; there were few firms large enough to take on the whole project until the 19th century. As a result most seemingly unified rows and crescents have slight differences to show where one builder finished and another started, or the same one at a later date.

STREETS AND ESTATES

Most new housing was erected upon geometrically designed layouts – squares, crescents, circles and in straight rows – the only meandering features usually coming from old roads or lanes that had been retained. There were few large-scale developments at first, the grandest projects being limited to one square or street at a time. The width of the roads in London and later in other cities was a reflection of the buildings along it, the taller and more expensive they were the wider the road (these proportions were enforced in London by Building Acts).

Most streets were poorly surfaced with no drainage and only in the best examples were there pavements to save pedestrians from the worst of the filth (foot-scrapers were an essential feature beside the door of most houses: see Fig

FIG 2.18 BEDFORD SQUARE, LONDON: *Many of the new streets or squares were named after the aristocratic owner of the land, whether or not he was directly involved in the development. Bedford Square was built in the 1770s for the Duke of Bedford.*

FIG 2.19: REGENTS PARK, LONDON: *One of the most ambitious schemes of the period was the rebuilding of part of the West End of London by John Nash for the Prince Regent (later George IV) with the construction of Regents Street and the Park. Grand, stucco-covered brick terraces were built along the main thoroughfare and around the new park.*

4.35). Later, larger terraces often had the road built up with the spoil from digging out the house foundations, leaving a basement below the street at the front but level with the garden on the original ground level at the rear. This also enabled the builder to provide storage under the pavement with coal chutes above for deliveries to be dropped down (see Fig 3.23).

By the early 19th century more ambitious schemes were undertaken, the most notable being Regents Street and Park by John Nash, which involved rebuilding a whole section of London's West End with a new main thorough-fare terminating in a grand park surrounded by classical terraces and pavilions. Some of the first large building firms also emerged, like that of Thomas Cubitt, which grew to employ a thousand men and whose clients would include Queen Victoria.

CHAPTER 3

The Georgian and Regency House

FIG 3.1 CHANDOS STREET, LONDON: *A street flanked by terraces laid out in the new suburbs of the West End of London in the late 18th century. Chandos House at the head of the road was built by Robert Adam in 1771 and faced with Craigleath stone from a quarry where he and his brother James had recently taken out a lease. Its restrained façade and delicate Neo Classical detailing on the portico and string courses are typical of his work.*

It's unlikely that when the king's baker, Thomas Farrinor, extinguished his oven on the evening of 1st September 1666 he would have realised that some tiny smouldering embers he had neglected to put out would start a chain of events that would play a large part in changing the face of housing in this country. The fire that spread from his premises over the

FIG 3.2 BUCKINGHAM: *A great fire swept through the small county town of Buckingham in 1725, destroying one in three houses. This late 18th century house was built after the devastation. The date of such events locally can help pinpoint the age of the houses subsequently rebuilt. Note also the bricked up windows on the top floor, which is often but not always due to an attempt to reduce the amount of window tax the owner had to pay.*

days and most towns, cities and even villages were regularly affected. The scale of this event, however, was such that the following year the first of many Building Acts was passed to ensure it did not happen again. These controlled the materials used, the method of construction and began standardising the size and design of houses, which, although only applying to London at first, subsequently became good practice elsewhere.

These changes gave rise to the end of individualistic local forms of housing, vernacular architecture, which was shaped by local geology with a builder's designs and methods passed down from father to son. Before examining the new materials and types of structure that dominated the Georgian period, it is worth briefly looking back at what came before – to put the new housing in context and particularly as some of it was still being built in these traditional styles during the 18th century.

following three days engulfed some 13,000 properties and wiped out the heart of the old City of London. Fires were an accepted part of life in those

Housing before 1700

During the Middle Ages houses were built by local craftsmen from locally available materials, and the majority

FIG 3.3: *The great fire of London and other conflagrations around the country encouraged householders to insure their properties against fire. New insurance companies were formed and as there were no numbers or house names, fire marks or metal badges, as in this example from Bath, were fixed to the front of houses covered. Each company had its own fire brigade and they would rush to the scene and attempt to extinguish the blaze, or if it was the wrong company they might leave it to burn! They lasted into the 19th century when local fire brigades began to be formed.*

were timber framed. Woodland was not the dark, foreboding place envisaged in Robin Hood or fairy tales, but was a well-managed commodity supplying timber for local building throughout the medieval, Tudor and Stuart periods. Earlier timber framed houses had thick members and wide spaces between; later the pieces were fitted more tightly in patterns or with close studded verticals, and by the 18th century those that were still built used thin, poorer quality wood, reflecting the low status of the owner and the lack of good supplies. The spaces between were usually infilled with wattle and daub, an interlaced surface of thin sticks or strips of wood (wattle) covered with a varying mix of mud, straw and other materials (daub) and then painted in sometimes bold and regionally varying colours and even patterns (pargeting) in some parts of East Anglia. This infill was sometimes replaced at a later date with brick, often laid in a diagonal, herringbone pattern.

In the Georgian period those who could not afford to completely rebuild could cover the exterior of their timber framed house with a new brick or stone façade. In the South East a popular alternative was to use horizontal timber boards, weatherboarding, or mathematical tiles, which hung off strips of wood laths like roof tiles to imitate brickwork.

Stone was an alternative but masonry was expensive due to the time and special skills required to quarry, prepare and transport it, while brick was only reintroduced in the later Middle Ages and then as a luxury

FIG 3.4: WELSH ROW, NANTWICH, CHESHIRE: *Timber-framed structures, as in the foreground, were replaced by more fire resistant brick structures, as in the rear of the picture. This also reflected the move to classical styling, which made a sudden and dramatic change to the structure of English houses in the 17th and 18th centuries.*

product for the rich. Rough stones or rubble were used for walls or just the footings of modest houses in areas where they could be easily extracted or collected, while cob (a similar mix to daub but dried out in blocks and stacked in thick walls with a protective white covering) was popular in Devon and parts of Buckinghamshire. With the growth in population and relative wealth there was an increase in building activity known as the Great Rebuilding, starting off in the later 16th century in the south and reaching the more remote northern and western areas in the 18th and 19th centuries. A larger number of people, successful merchants and traders in towns and yeoman farmers in the country, could afford more permanent houses built of local stone and brick. However, much of the new housing continued to be timber framed, even in London where this had been banned from 1605.

By the 18th century the new building regulations, changing fashions and the declining number and quality of trees, due to increased shipbuilding, made timber framed structures rare and usually only for poorer rural housing. However, the improved road and river transport later in the century caused other materials to become cheaper and more widely available and new ideas and fashions could be more rapidly spread. Standardisation of elements like bricks and sash windows and the avail-ability of well designed and fashionable houses in pattern books meant that the same house could be built in any part of the country although variation in local stone or the colour of bricks still gave it some regionalisation. Other elements of vernacular architecture were retained, especially in details like metalwork, which were still supplied by local craftsmen, and bricks, which were made at local works, but for most of the houses featured in this book their appearance was guided by national fashions and trends rather than by regional traditions.

Materials

STONE

The most desirable material for houses was stone, especially finely cut masonry

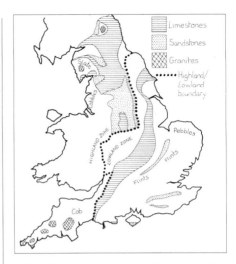

FIG 3.5: *A map of England showing the main areas where sandstones, limestones and granites were used for house building, with additional captions highlighting places where other excavated materials could be found.*

or ashlar. Accurately squared blocks of limestone and sandstone with the narrowest of joints produced a permanent, fireproof and refined exterior that suited the classical taste of the time. Larger scale quarrying and improved transport had by the 18th century made stone more widely available, being used for even cheaper terrace housing in areas close to extraction but only better quality houses further away. In most ordinary houses built of stone, rubble or irregular blocks were used, which with a partly cut or completely rough surface was cheaper. It was also common for the façade of better houses to be finished in ashlar but the sides

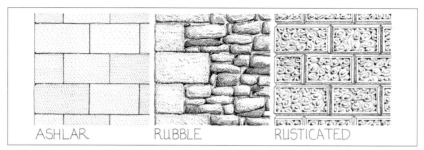

FIG 3.6: *Three finishes of stone. Ashlar was common on the finest houses, rubble could be found down the sides and back of the same houses or on cheaper buildings, and rusticated was a finish often carved out for the lower storey of Palladian styled houses and imitated later in stucco on many Regency buildings.*

and other walls to be built from rubble to save costs.

Limestone was used in some of the most notable Georgian buildings. It is a sedimentary rock, that is one made from sediments built up over millennia in prehistoric seas with the type of deposits and tiny creatures trapped within determining its characteristics (for instance Oolitic limestone, which is used in the Cotswolds, is named after tiny sea creatures called oolites within it). Later impurities gave them their various colours. Portland stone, a greyish limestone, was used in some of our finest buildings, the creamy coloured Bath stone was used in this city and surrounding areas, rusty yellow to brown stone is distinctive of the Cotswolds, Oxfordshire and Northamptonshire, while steel grey limestone was used further north in the Peak District and Pennines.

Sandstone is also sedimentary but formed with deposits of fine rock particles in ancient desert conditions or river deltas, making a soft, less durable rock but with great variations in texture. One of the hardest types was millstone grit containing particles of minerals like quartz, which were found in the Peak District and South Pennines, but there were many other softer types widely used in building in areas like Carlisle and the North East,

FIG 3.7: *Although many houses appear to be of solid stone, the ashlar façade in this example is only a veneer with cheaper brick used for the main part of the wall.*

FIG 3.8: *Smaller and softer stones like the flint in the left-hand picture and clunch, a hard chalk, on the right needed brickwork to make the corners and sometimes form horizontal bands in the wall.*

Lancashire and Cheshire, Sussex, the West Midlands and Shropshire.

Both of these stones were relatively easily cut and shaped using saws and chisels and are referred to as freestones. Harder igneous rocks (those that are formed from ancient flows of magma) are generally termed granites and are mainly found in wall construction in Cornwall, Devon and Cumbria.

In areas with poor supplies of these building stones and suitable timber,

other deposits were used. Flints, very hard dark-grey irregular nodules found in chalk, were the main component for walls in parts of East Anglia and southern England where the chalk it is found in is near the surface, although red brick made up the corners and openings. Clunch, a harder type of chalk, was used in a similar way in the same areas. Pebbles found along south and eastern coastal regions and larger cobbles in the North West and Humberside were also

FIG 3.9: BEDFORD SQUARE, LONDON: *If you could not use the real thing, then artificial stone was available, the most notable being Coade stone used for details like capitals and keystones or whole doorways as in this example. It was sold by Eleanor Coade from 1769 to her death in 1821 and although it continued to be made for a few decades afterwards, its composition remained a secret although it is now believed to be a type of ceramic.*

used. In this period these irregular stones were generally utilised in the cheaper terraces and cottages.

STUCCO

If you could not afford the real thing, then you could apply a render to your house so it appeared to be of stone. During the late 18th century and Regency period a wide variety of renders were available although they are all generally referred to as stucco. Most were types of cements patented and marketed under titles like Roman Cement or Portland Cement, the latter patented in 1824 and named as such because it imitated the fashionable grey Portland stone. It was used sometimes just for details on the façade, other times for the ground floor, with deep horizontal lines to imitate rough hewn stone found in the base of classical temples. It became more widespread in the early 19th century as a covering for the whole house, some with fine lines to imply ashlar masonry, and can still be found in spa towns such as Cheltenham, seaside resorts such as Brighton and most notably in Nash's Regents Park development. Although most houses are now painted in whites and creams, at the time the finish was more likely to be in a more subdued beige or grey to match the colour of the quality stone it sought to imitate.

The problem with stucco is that not all variants worked and some fell off after a short period. It could also be

Fig 3.10: *Houses might have just the lower storey covered in stucco (left) or the entire façade (right).*

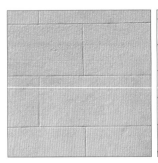

FIG 3.11: *The surface of the render could simply be incised with narrow lines imitating fine masonry (left), formed with deep horizontal grooves to create a rusticated base to the house (middle) or left plain with the stucco used to make decorative features like the frieze and cornice (right).*

used to cover up a wall of poor quality construction and the use of cheap bricks behind it gave it a bad reputation in many people's eyes.

BRICKS

The most popular material for houses was brick. No longer was it a luxury product for the finest gentry houses, its widespread use gave permanence and fireproofing to all levels of housing, although the quality varied. Bricks were produced locally, mostly at a growing number of brickworks, but sometimes they were made on the site of the house from clay dug in the imme-diate area, as had been the traditional way. The content of the clay, its prep-aration and position in the kiln affected the properties of the brick. Good quality bricks, which were required for the fine jointed work on the front of a house, demanded the best clay, with unwanted impurities removed, and they were fired in the hottest part of the kiln. Less well fired and poorer quality

products were used for side and internal walls while overheated bricks, which turned grey/blue, could be used in decorative patterns.

Soft bricks known as rubbers were also important as they could be sanded down or carved to produce fine decorative work like the lintels above windows. Regional variations in the clay resulted in different colour bricks, for instance deep reds in Staffordshire, yellow stock bricks in London, greys around Reading and paler off-whites in Cambridgeshire. Red brick had been the fashionable choice in the previous century and continued to be widely used in this period but after around 1750, builders, especially in London, preferred colours such as beiges, creams or greys which imitated stone.

Bricks were hand-made so the finished shape is not always as sharp edged as the later 19th century types. Bricks from around 1800, and increasingly so in the Victorian period, had a recess called a frog on the top or

FIG 3.12: *Rubbers were fine quality bricks that could be sanded down to make precisely shaped forms like this arch, with the narrowest gaps between them.*

on both top and bottom, which is useful to note if dating walls as earlier bricks were usually flat surfaced. Size had varied in early brick buildings but in the 17th century dimensions of 9" x 4" x 3" were generally adopted. In order to raise money in the wake of the American War of Independence a brick tax was levied on the total number used in a house from 1784. It was therefore an advantage if the brick was larger – to reduce the overall quantity and hence the amount levied – and larger bricks up to 10 inches long were produced (brick tax was abolished in 1851).

Bonding was the arrangement of the bricks in the wall, creating different patterns of headers (the short end of the brick) and stretchers (the long side) on the exposed surface. Flemish bond was the most popular, with alternate headers and stretchers along each course or layer of bricks; in cheaper variations a number of courses of stretchers between one of mixed was inserted, reducing the number of bricks used. English bond had fallen from favour and was not widely used until its revival in the late 19th century, while header bond was needed to produce smooth curves, as on bay windows.

The mortar between the bricks was

FIG 3.13: *Bricks from this period were hand-made so have slightly rough textures and edges, unlike later Victorian machine-made types, which have a more consistent surface and sharper corners. The surface of the example on the right has worn away to reveal the impurities that remain from the original clay, a local character lacking in mass-produced bricks.*

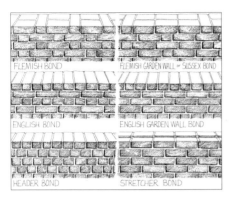

FIG 3.14: *Sections of wall showing the outer surface pattern and the arrangement of brick in the wall of the different bonds. Flemish bond and the garden wall variant, where extra stretchers were inserted to reduce costs, were the most popular. English and stretcher bonds are rare in this period, while header bond was generally only used to create curved walls in a bow or bay window.*

FIG 3.15: *An example of tuck pointing where the rough edged bricks with wide joints had the mortar coloured to match the brick (the irregular dark grey lines in the photo). A thin bead of lime putty was then inserted into it to give the impression of fine jointed brickwork.*

usually lime-based throughout this period although some cement-based types did appear in the Regency era. Although not as strong as cement mortars, lime-based types allow moisture to pass through and this property matched by the bricks of the age means that the walls in effect breathe, an important thing to remember when repairing old houses as modern products do not, and can damage brickwork if used. Pointing is the visible finish of the mortar on the face of the wall and in this period was usually flush with the brickwork. When good quality bricks were used the gap between them could be very fine, where cheaper bricks

with uneven shape or rough edges were used the gap was larger. There were methods in the trade to make a house look more refined: one type was tuck pointing, where the wet mortar was coloured to match the surrounding brick and a fine line was incised into it and filled with light coloured mortar so that it looked as if better quality bricks had been used (see Fig 3.15).

General Structure

The construction of the main structure of the house became increasingly controlled by Building Acts throughout the Georgian period. The early legislation going back to the previous century was for London but often became good practice elsewhere. The main change was the exclusive use of stone and brick for the external walls and the removal of wooden features such as exposed sash boxes and cornices from the face of the building so that fire could not spread easily from house to house. It was the 1774 Building Act drafted by leading architects that first aimed to control the standard of construction and fire prevention nationwide. Despite the elegant appearance of Georgian houses many were poorly built and complete collapse was not uncommon, so this new legislation not only imposed more stringent guidelines for fire prevention but also attempted some form of quality control. Cheap materials, shallow foundations and poor methods of construction were still to be found, especially on the small terraces and back to backs of the working classes, which were being erected in increasing quantity after this Act. The term 'jerry building' (from a nautical term for temporary rigging) was first coined in the Regency period to describe the shortcuts still made by builders at all levels of housing.

WALLS AND FLOORS

Brick and masonry walls of this date are nearly always solid with only small gaps, depending on the bonding, and not with a cavity as in more modern housing. The depth was around 9 inches, the length of a single brick, on smaller houses but in medium and larger terraces it was thicker than this on the lower floors, around 2 to 2½ bricks deep, tapering away as it reached the attic where it was usually 1 brick deep. It was also common for the quality bricks used on the façade to be only a thin veneer, with the main body

of the wall behind constructed of cheaper versions (see Fig 3.16), as was typical on stone and stucco-faced terraces. Party and rear walls, which were out of sight, were also constructed from these cheaper bricks.

Internal divisions were only usually of brick where they had to carry a

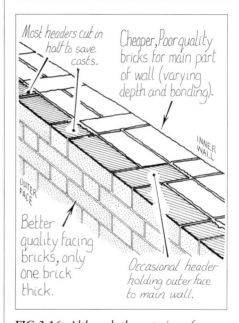

FIG 3.16: *Although the exterior of a house may appear to have been built from fine quality bricks, builders who were always looking for ways of cutting costs often used these more expensive types as an outer facing, with the main body of the wall constructed from cheaper types. In this example most of the headers on the outer face have been cut in half as a further economy measure, with just the occasional full length one to tie the outer and inner parts together.*

substantial load, at the lower levels or as a main load-bearing wall in larger houses. Most walls inside the house were made from a timber frame with laths and plaster applied (see Fig 5.17 – plaster and laths on brick). Foundations were often shallow, with the brickwork splaying out at the base, and there was rarely any form of damp course in the lower stages of the wall above. Basements were common in medium and large houses and offered some protection against damp, especially when the kitchen fireplace was sited there.

Floors could be solid at ground level (sometimes even where there was a basement below, which would have a brick, vaulted ceiling to support the floor above) with a marble or other polished stone surface in the finest houses. In the cheapest houses it might be no more than quarry tiled, or composed of bricks on end, or in some just beaten earth. Most floors in the house consisted of wooden joists running from one side to the other and resting upon steps or sockets in the walls, with the planks nailed at right angles on top (you can always tell the direction of hidden joists as they will be at right angles to the floorboards). The floorboards tend to be wide at this date, although thinner boards could be seen in better quality and later houses, with pine from the Baltics becoming widespread towards the end of the period.

WINDOWS AND DOORS

The principal change to the structure of windows and doors in this period came from the imposition of fire regulations and the use of the relatively new sash

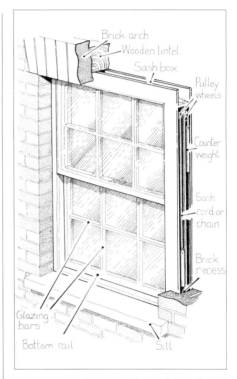

FIG 3.17: *A drawing of a sash window showing its inner workings and how it was recessed behind the outer brickwork after the 1774 Building Act.*

window. Devised in the late 17th century in England and the Netherlands, the vertical sliding sash window gave a flexible way of controlling ventilation throughout the seasons as well as proportions that were best suited to the new classical styled façades that were becoming fashionable. The two sashes, wooden frames subdivided by glazing bars, were set within slots in an outer box (sash box) so that they could be raised

FIG 3.18: *The left hand example shows an earlier sash window flush with the wall, as could still be found in some early Georgian houses. The example in the central picture is recessed back 4 inches but with the outer box still exposed, as first imposed in London in 1709. The right hand example is fitted as dictated by the 1774 Building Act, with the box hidden behind the brick wall. Note also how the later example has finer glazing bars.*

or dropped independently of each other by pulleys and weights hidden within (see Fig 3.17). In smaller housing the sashes were not usually hung but held in place by wedges or slid horizontally, especially on top floors (Yorkshire sash, see Fig 4.31.2, 4.31.4 and 4.31.18).

Originally the sash box was exposed at the front but an Act of 1709 forced builders, at first only in London, to set it back at least four inches from the face of the wall. The later 1774 Act took it a stage further and set the sash box back behind the outer wall to further reduce fire risk.

The imposition of window tax led many builders and owners to build brick recesses in place of glazing or to block up existing openings to reduce the total number of windows by which the tax was calculated (it varied through the period, being imposed on houses with more than 6 to 8 windows before it was repealed in 1851). Be aware, though, that many windows were left blocked because it was convenient for the room behind and not because of the tax; it would have been top floor or rear windows that were more likely to be blocked for tax purposes (see Fig 3.2).

The front door surround was also affected by this legislation as the wooden surrounds and hoods that were still popular on some houses were banned as part of fire prevention. This, coupled with changing fashion, created the plain entrance with the only decoration in the semi-circular fanlight above the door, which became characteristic of later Georgian terraces, with stone (real and artificial) or stucco-covered brick used to make classical surrounds on the finest houses. Later Regency entrances were further enlivened with the use of decorative ironwork balconies or extended porches supported on columns (porticos). See Fig 4.28 – Fig 4.31 for examples and styles of windows and doors.

ROOFS

Georgian detached houses posed a problem in roofing their new larger structure. Most houses in medieval and Tudor times had been built as single properties even if they butted up to others to form a continuous row. These were composed of units one room deep, as the steep pitch required to support the roof materials of the time, clay tile or thatch, could not spread beyond that without complicated and expensive trusses. In the late 17th century, however, and throughout the Georgian period the double pile house, two rooms deep, was built. The solution to the roofing issue was to still use steeper pitched roofs wide enough to overlay one room but set them either parallel, one behind the other, or in a ring to cover the wider structure. This created a problem with the valley where the two pitches met, a notorious weak point for rain to enter, which needed constant attention and maintenance. By the later

FIG 3.19: *The end gable of a double pile house showing the two separate pitched roofs, which run parallel across the structure (top). The central valley was lead-lined to collect the rainwater and, if they wanted to avoid gutters down the façade, gulleys could run from the front behind the parapet, through the first gabled roof and into the valley. The second view is of a later slate-covered Regency roof, which due to its lighter weight could span the whole in one.*

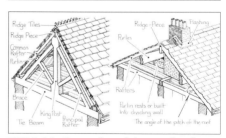

FIG 3.20: *Examples of the inside of a pitched roof. On the left is a king post truss, one of the types of truss that support and spread the weight of the structure. On the right is an arrangement used on terraces where the two large purlins running halfway up the slope of the roof rest upon the dividing walls between each house.*

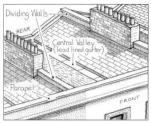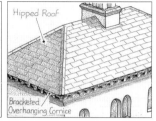

FIG 3.21: *Examples of other types of roofs to be found on Georgian and Regency houses.*

18th century, however, lighter Welsh slate became more widely available and the whole double pile could be covered by one shallow pitched roof.

Similar problems existed for larger terraces where the roofs usually ran front to back, with the central valley above the centre of the house. This was hidden from the road below by a parapet, another feature of fire prevention to avoid flames getting to the roof timbers, but one that also suited the classical style of the façade. The introduction of slate again gave more flexibility in the design of the roof. Another type of roof that became increasingly popular on larger terraces was the mansard where the slope of the roof is made up of a steep and then a shallow pitch, creating more height within for an attic.

Types of House

The houses of the well-off Georgian could come in various shapes and sizes, from large detached villas and towering terraces in the towns and cities to stout square farmhouses and vicarages in the country. Despite these differences the basic principles of the interior layout, especially in terraces, was fairly fixed

throughout the period. In the past, the main reception rooms had been on the ground floor and in larger houses even the principal bedchambers, but as the Palladian style became popular in the early to mid 18th century so these important rooms could be found on the first floor, raised above a rusticated ground level. The windows and ceilings were higher on this floor, the piano

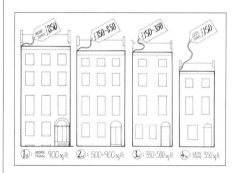

FIG 3.22: *It was another aspect of first the 1667 Rebuilding Act for London and then the 1774 Building Act that urban houses were categorised by area and value into differing rates. In the later legislation First Rate was the largest and Fourth Rate the smallest (the values are of the building costs and the sizes are the total area of all the rooms together).*

nobile, to emphasise its importance. In terraces the main rooms were split between the ground and first floor so as to create a similar effect. The lower level had a rusticated treatment on the exterior and contained the day to day rooms for the family while the new piano nobile above was raised in height (the ceiling height may have been the same as the ground floor but the windows were taller) to make an imposing drawing room and dining room above the noise and dirt of the street below. There was usually a balcony to overlook the front (rarely the back) with full height sash windows (French windows became popular in the 1830s and sometimes replaced the earlier sashes) or just ironwork guards across the openings in smaller houses.

It was also typical at this date for most of the service rooms to be in the basement. Early examples tended to be fully subterranean with, on the finest houses, an open area in front with steps leading down to it, a feature that became increasingly widespread from the mid 18th century. Half basements with steps leading up to a slightly elevated ground floor, which made the entrance look more impressive and cast more light into the floor below, became popular from the late Georgian period. This also reduced the depth for excavation although in many urban terraces the basement floor actually stood on the real ground level and it was the road at the front that was built up with the spoil from building. In medium-sized houses there may have only been a light well at the front with access from inside or the rear. The

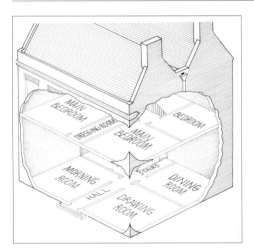
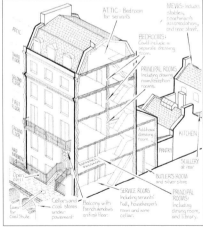

FIG 3.23: *Cut away plans of a detached Georgian double pile house (left) and a large Regency terrace (right). Notice on the later example how the kitchen and scullery have been moved out into the rear yard now that piped water was available to create more room in the basement for a larger suite of service rooms.*

FIG 3.24: *The basement of larger terraces was accessed down the steps through the 'area' at the front of the house. The left hand example dates from around 1740 with a full depth basement so the front door is level with the street; the right hand picture shows a later type with just a half basement so the front door is now up a set of steps, making a more imposing entrance. On smaller terraces there may have been no area and just a light well to illuminate the basement (see Fig 3.26).*

kitchen would have been positioned down here, with its fireplace usually up against a party wall in terraces, giving off heat all day, which must in part have reduced the problem with damp. Although there were often further service rooms at the rear in larger houses, it was not until the Victorian period that better accommodation for staff was provided.

Another development in the design of terraces was the appearance of the row as a whole. As most houses were built in small groups by small-scale builders, large-scale planning may have been limited to general rules on appearance, size and position dictated by local implementation of Building Acts or by the landlord. In these larger and fashionable developments the row could be treated as one architectural piece. Palace-fronted terraces, where the ends and central dwellings are emphasised to give the whole the appearance of a large country house either in a straight row or crescent, were popular from the mid 18th century through to the end of the Regency period. Another common distinction of the Georgian and Regency terrace is that the front door was positioned on the same side of each house in a row, whereas in smaller buildings and in later Victorian houses it became fashionable for the doors to be set in pairs.

FIG 3.25: QUEEN SQUARE, BATH: *A palace-fronted terrace with the end and centre elements projecting to give the impression that the whole takes the form of a country house.*

FIG 3.27: *A semi-detached and linked house with the doors set in a smaller side block, creating more room on the ground floor.*

FIG 3.26: *A row of terraced houses from Liverpool with their front doors on the same side of each property rather than cheaper and later Victorian dwellings where they were usually paired together.*

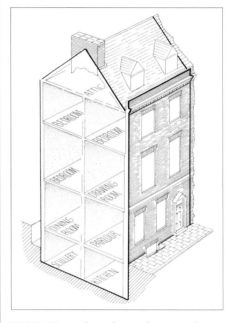

FIG 3.28: *A plan of a medium-sized terrace house from the late Georgian period.*

Despite being associated with 20th century mass housing, the urban semi-detached house first appeared as a distinctive form in the late 18th century alongside fashionable villas and terraces on the then outskirts of towns and in seaside and spa resorts. They could take on the appearance of a row of terraced houses with gaps between or two linked detached dwellings. A distinctive form in the Regency period was to have a lower unit set back from the façade containing the front door at each side of a semi or at the end of a small row of terrace houses (see Fig 3.27).

WORKING CLASS TERRACES

There were also distinctive types of terrace built for the growing urban workforce, although it would have been only those fortunate enough to live in a well paid area (for instance you could earn twice as much in a Lancashire mill town than in some rural towns in the south) or to be in a senior or specialised position who could afford the rent on a small terraced property. They could range from a modest two up two down through house (with a front and rear door opening directly into the rooms) with separate bedrooms for the children and parents, down to back to backs set in rows or around courtyards with a single room above and below and possibly a cellar for storage. Although these houses, which were often squeezed in at the rear of larger properties or in haphazard developments, were later to become the slums of the Victorian period, many did provide decent accommodation at the time, often an improvement over damp hovels back in the country.

Another distinctive type was the weavers' terraced house where living rooms and bedrooms were on the ground and first floors with an open second floor above, lit by elongated windows to cast light on the workplace.

FIG 3.29: *A small terraced through house from the early 19th century with two ground floor rooms and two upstairs bedrooms. Where they stand today, a bathroom has usually been inserted into one of the bedrooms, leaving a small space for a box room. They do not tend to have rear extensions at this date, only a small yard or garden.*

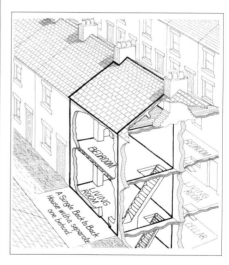

FIG 3.30: *A cut away drawing of a back to back house with a cellar, living room and bedroom stacked upon each other and no access to the side or rear.*

CHAPTER 4

Georgian and Regency Style

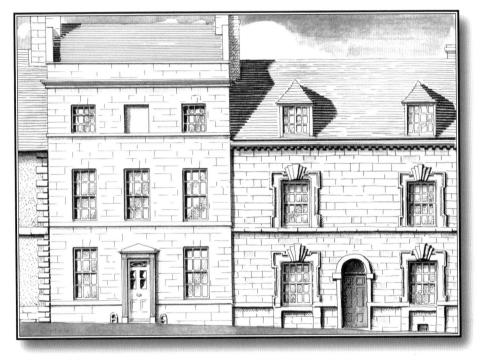

FIG 4.1: STAMFORD, LINCOLNSHIRE: *Differing styles of stone Georgian houses. The right hand example is an earlier type with gabled roof and dormer windows; the left hand example is influenced by the new, more austere Palladian style and emphasises the vertical, with a parapet hiding the roof and plain window openings.*

The style of Georgian and Regency houses was dominated by classical architecture. The proportions, dimensions and detailing of the façade were based upon the orders from Ancient Greece and Rome, reinterpreted by later architects and made available to even the humble builder through numerous and detailed pattern books. The architectural quality of even the small terrace owes much to these valuable publications, which the master mason, bricklayer or carpenter would have used to guide construction. In the late 17th and early 18th century, with poor communication and little travel, changes in fashions in the building trade took time to reach more remote areas; the latest style in London could take up to fifty years to reach the most remote parts of the country. There were also local types of window or door surround and decorative features that may have only appeared in that area or persisted in a locality long after they had gone out of fashion elsewhere. However, with the growth of architecture as a trade, improved transport and the widespread availability of these pattern books, the time delay for fashions to spread begins to evaporate and local styles fade as houses become standardised.

As a country, however, we generally lagged behind the Continent before this period and it was in 15th-century Italy that the rebirth of classical architecture, the Renaissance, became prominent, at a time when nobles back here were still constructing rambling timber framed houses. Leading architects created new forms of domestic architecture based upon the classical orders of Ancient Rome, the most notable being Andrea Palladio (1508–80). Through a study of the remains of Roman buildings and an understanding of proportions he created a distinctive style of domestic building that has become known as Palladian. His most notable achievement, however, was the book *I quattro libri dell'architettura*, a self publicising piece of literature in which he recorded

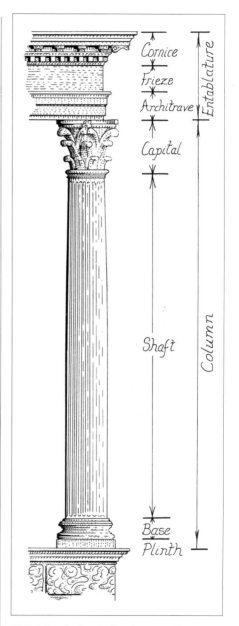

FIG 4.2: *A classical column and entablature with labels of its parts.*

Cornice

Frieze

Architrave

Entablature

Capital

Shaft

Column

Base

Plinth

FIG 4.3: THE CLASSICAL ORDERS: *Each order had different proportions and style of entablature and capital at the top of the column. The Roman orders pictured here (from left to right), 1: Composite, 2: Corinthian, 3: Ionic and 4: Roman Doric/Tuscan, were used from before the Georgian period as they had been studied from the Renaissance onwards, and feature on early – and some later – Georgian houses. The Greek orders, however, were not recorded accurately until the mid 18th century and hence grew in popularity later in the period (see Fig 4.11).*

FIG 4.4: WINSLOW HALL, BUCKINGHAMSHIRE: *One of the few houses that is likely to have been designed by Sir Christopher Wren, dating from the first decade of the 18th century. It displays many of the features that were popular on similar high quality houses of the day – a hipped roof with a wooden cornice below, red brick walls with stone quoins, and a segmental arched door surround.*

his theories, and which was to become influential to later Georgian architects.

Early attempts at classical architecture in this country were done with little understanding of the rules of proportion and composition. Tudor and Stuart houses tend to have columns and detailing affixed to standard structures in a sometimes amateurish way. A notable exception was the work, mainly for the Crown, of Inigo Jones (1573–1652) who, after visiting Italy, where he was profoundly influenced by the work of Palladio, returned to these shores and created the first true classical buildings. He was, however, way ahead of his time and after the Restoration in 1660 it was the domestic style of the Low Countries, where many Royalists had been based throughout the Commonwealth and from where William of Orange came in 1688, that shaped building in the late 17th century. By the opening of the Georgian period, houses were still being built under the influence of Dutch architecture and that watered down Baroque style popularised by Sir Christopher Wren (St Paul's Cathedral), Sir John Vanbrugh (Blenheim Palace) and Nicholas Hawksmoor.

Early Georgian Styles 1714–1760

Large red bricked houses with white cornices and dormer windows, stone houses with moulded framed windows and flamboyant Baroque shell hoods and terraces with segmental arched windows and red brick dressing were still the common form when George I ascended the throne. Although in London these styles had fallen from favour by the 1730s they remained popular or formed eclectic mixes with later styles in other parts of the country.

It was the classical style of Ancient Rome reinterpreted by Palladio that spread to affect most levels of housing in the first half of the 18th century. The change was fuelled in part by young nobles venturing to Italy, among other destinations, on Grand Tours designed as part of their education but often ending up as a shopping spree for ancient relics. Upon their return they wanted new houses to store their collections of antiquities and the new Palladian style met with their approval now they had seen the originals for themselves. There was also political influence as the Whigs, who had risen to power with the new monarch, sought a national style. They rejected the Baroque as too French, too Tory and hence by association Jacobite, and

under the influence of Richard Boyle, 3rd Earl of Burlington, who controlled appointments to key architectural posts, encouraged the development of the Palladian style (see Fig 1.1). The other key character was Colen Campbell who translated the works of the Roman architect and engineer Vitruvius and, including his own designs and those of Inigo Jones,

FIG 4.5: BROOK STREET, LONDON: *An example of a terrace in the style of Wren and typical of the turn of the 18th century and early Georgian period. It has segmental arches above windows, red brick dressing and string course and box sashes exposed to the front. The large pilasters at the extremities of the façade were also a popular Baroque feature. This house was the home of Handel for twenty-five years and then two hundred years later Jimmy Hendrix moved in next door!*

FIG 4.6: BURLINGTON STREET, LONDON: *Built between 1718 and 1723 by Colen Campbell, these new terraces were designed on Palladian rules. The façade was based on the classical temple, with the lower string course marking the top of the plinth and the cornice at the top the top of the entablature.*

the ground floor acting as the base either by a rusticated finish to the masonry or with a string course along its top edge, and a further string course to mark the entablature above the second floor. There was an element of honesty to the style as interior use was emphasised on the outside with the largest windows on the first floor, the new piano nobile, where the main reception rooms were. Most façades were plain but some had moulded

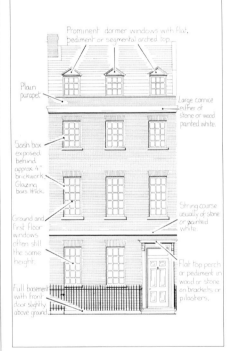

FIG 4.7: *A Second Rate terrace (see Fig 3.22) from the early Georgian period displaying some of the features that were characteristic of larger houses in this period.*

created the basis of an anglicised version of the ancient forms.

Palladian houses relied on correct proportions for the composition of the façade with little decoration other than the doorway surround. The temples of the Ancients, with a rustic cut stone base upon which the columns stood, carrying the entablature above, were transmuted to the domestic house, with

FIG 4.8: *Examples of a terrace and a large rural detached house in a Palladian style.*

FIG 4.9: GIBBS SURROUNDS: *James Gibbs was another proponent of Palladian style who visited Italy initially to train for the priesthood but returned an architect. He published books that made the style accessible to the builder rather than architects but he is best known for the door and window surround with distinctive spaced blocks which he popularised.*

window surrounds and door cases with flat, segmented or pedimented tops.

Later Georgian Styles 1760–1800

In the second half of the 18th century the austere, refined, elegant Palladian style continued to dominate housing stock, especially terraces. The façade was still controlled by rules on proportion and a desire for symmetry. Window glazing bars became thinner and sash boxes from 1774 were hidden fully behind the outer face of the wall. Exterior woodwork was banned so porches were less frequently fitted unless of stone or stucco and decorative semi-circular fanlights became very popular. Cornices at the top (no longer of timber) and the parapet above tend to be more simple and plain although decorative stone or stucco cornices were fitted to the finest examples.

There were subtle changes, however, as a new generation of architects looked not to Ancient and Renaissance Italy for inspiration but to newly recorded buildings from Ancient Greece. Larger houses were no longer based purely upon the designs of Palladio; instead they were sourced directly from archaeology and archi-

FIG 4.10: *Examples of houses from the second half of the 18th century including features that were popular in this period, such as bay and Venetian windows, façades that were less decorative and large fanlights.*

FIG 4.11: *The new records of Ancient Greek architecture resulted in forms that were earlier than the Roman types becoming popular especially the Greek Doric (left) with its fluted column and the Ionic (right).*

tects had a greater freedom to mix different periods into one house. James 'Athenian' Stuart and Nicholas Revett were among the first to publish their studies in the 1760s, heralding in a more refined form of decoration, but sometimes severe and stark structural forms like the baseless Doric column (see Fig 4.11). This Greek revival had little effect on the design of urban houses until the last decades of the century and tends to appear on the terrace only in the design for columns on a doorway or in a band of decoration.

The most popular and influential architect of this period was Robert Adam who, along with his brother, created a unique style that gave patrons more varied and decorative structures, without being too austere like the Greek Revivalists or breaking with traditional symmetry when using Gothick forms. He was one of the first to design the house in its entirety, from the exterior down to the smallest detail, and was notable for his interiors, especially his use of screens and niches to control the space within a room. His style is recognisable on the exterior of houses by the use of shallow mouldings for decoration in bands across a façade or around a porch entablature, swags or garlands and round medallions. He also had a preference for Venetian windows and shallow arched recesses, which added variety to the design, and

FIG 4.12: *Details from houses in the Adam brothers' style with their distinctive delicate, shallow mouldings.*

doorways that had sidelights, engaged columns and fanlights covering the whole.

Regency Styles 1790–1837

At the same time as these new forms of classical architecture were appearing, a new concept and source for design was evolving. This was to lead to a greater variety of architectural styles, which is characteristic of the Regency period. The country was boosted by a growing empire and industry and sought a national identity, one that was home

FIG 4.13: *A façade of a house designed by James Wyatt, one of the leading architects of the late 18th century and a rival of Robert Adam, with labels highlighting some of the fashionable features used at the time.*

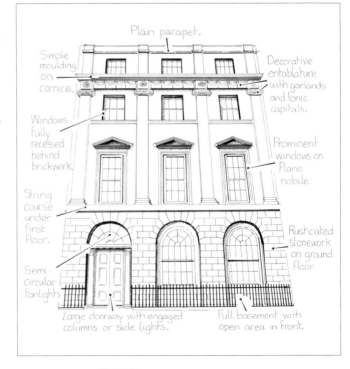

Plain parapet.

Simple moulding on cornice.

Decorative entablature with garlands and Ionic capitals.

Windows fully recessed behind brickwork.

Prominent windows on Piano nobile

String course under first floor.

Rusticated stonework on ground floor

Semi-circular fanlights

Large doorway with engaged columns or side lights.

Full basement with open area in front.

grown and not set in the ancient world, and the answer came from the landscape. In the past the countryside was viewed more as a factory floor with fields, rivers and forests providing essential materials and food, with any mountainous areas viewed with disdain. However, in the middle of the 18th century, a new way of thinking and looking at the surrounding landscape developed and the drama and beauty of the English countryside were appreciated for the first time. Improved coaches and new turnpike roads meant that previously remote areas like the Peak District, Lake District and Scotland could be easily visited and new guidebooks suddenly appeared on the market, especially after the outbreak of the Napoleonic Wars brought an end to the Grand Tours and foreign travel.

Along with this Picturesque movement came a growing appreciation for medieval architecture. Ruined abbeys had been seen as bleak and Catholic and were hence unloved, but now they were appreciated as the work of God and were painted and recreated in landscape gardens. Castles with their rugged appearance clashed with the fashionable and symmetrical classical buildings, yet by the turn of the century a wave of patriotism had been inspired in the wake of the threat from France, and sham fortified country houses

FIG 4.14: LOWTHER CASTLE, CUMBRIA: *In the early years of the 19th century mock castles and country houses decorated with battlements were built, partly due to the Picturesque movement but also as a patriotic reaction to the threat from Napoleon.*

began to be built. The effects of these new aesthetics on housing was freedom with structural planning so that buildings could be asymmetrical, different styles and sources could be assimilated onto one building and designs based upon the medieval pointed arch became fashionable.

Gothick, as it was termed to differentiate it from the later Victorian Gothic (which was a more accurate representation of medieval architec-

FIG 4.15: *Details from Gothick style houses with the distinctive Y-shaped glazing bars, battlements, shallow pointed arches and stucco-covered exteriors.*

ture), is characterised by shallow pointed arched windows and doors with tracery forming Y shapes and drip moulds above them. Solid or battlemented parapets on gables, white stucco-covered exteriors, and prominent Tudor styled chimneys also featured although the main body of the house may still have been symmetrical. It was popular for detached villas, smaller houses on country estates and gatehouses, and details from the style – such as the windows – can sometimes be found on terrace housing. Another variation of Olde English architecture was the Cottage Orné style, over romanticised chocolate box cottages with thatched roofs, designed for the middle classes on the edge of town rather than to improve the standard of often still woeful rural housing.

The simple style of Ancient Greek architecture, which had first been recorded back in the 1760s, came into fashion. The Neo Classical style could be stark and in the hands of architects like Sir John Soane (see Fig 2.3) almost modern in its simple geometric forms. For most housing this Greek Revival meant the use of the Greek Ionic and Doric orders. Contact with far-flung parts of the empire also resulted in an assimilation of their styles, rarely in the design of a whole structure but in the decoration and details. Chinese pagoda style roofs were commonly fitted to balconies and discoveries from Ancient Egypt resulted in the occasional decorative motif or tapered pilaster.

For the vast majority of detached and terrace housing a distinctive

FIG 4.16: *Cottage Orné was a type of pretty, quaint, usually thatched cottage style, as in this example, but was designed for wealthy occupants who looked for new Picturesque style building in the fashionable suburbs and countryside rather than for rural folk.*

Regency style developed incorporating elements from all the above styles and new forms from France and Italy. The most notable feature was the use of stucco on the exterior; although commonly painted white or cream today, it was more usual at that time for it to be coloured to simulate the popular grey and beige stone of the day. The increased availability of slate meant that low pitched roofs with overhangs and no parapet became popular on housing.

The use of decorative ironwork on the exterior, especially the balcony, was another distinctive and widespread feature. Half basements became common and so the ground floor was raised up with a set of steps, stucco-covered brick or stone porches supported on columns (porticos) were also popular. On smaller houses semi-circular fanlights remained in vogue, many having the distinctive reeded

FIG 4.17: *Details from houses in a Greek Revival style.*

FIG 4.18: **EDENSOR DERBYSHIRE:** *Rural estate housing broke with formal design of earlier work (see Fig 2.16) and became more picturesque, inspired by designs from books like John Loudon's 'Encyclopaedia of Cottage, Farm and Villa Architecture' of 1833. These details of houses from Edensor were inspired by this book, and feature clockwise from the top left medieval battlements, Mock Tudor timber framing, Norman blind arcading and Italian villas.*

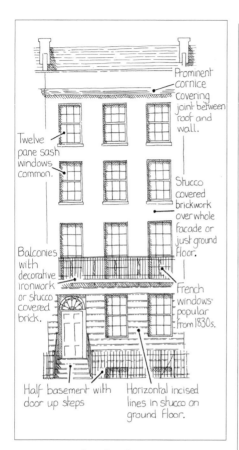

Prominent cornice covering joint between roof and wall.

Twelve pane sash windows common.

Stucco covered brickwork over whole facade or just ground floor.

Balconies with decorative ironwork or stucco covered brick.

French windows popular from 1830s.

Half basement with door up steps

Horizontal incised lines in stucco on ground floor.

FIG 4.19: *A façade of a Regency terrace, highlighting some of the fashionable features.*

moulding that was used inside and out on Regency houses and usually continued up over the arch at the top of a door.

Windows became even more elegant with metal used to strengthen the glazing bars enabling them to become as thin as possible, with large panes of glass and taller windows on the

FIG 4.20: *Although stucco was widespread, stone and exposed brick were still used. Note the raised half basement and Ionic capitals on the brick example from Liverpool (top) and the iron balconies and window guards on the others from Stamford (middle) and Cheltenham (bottom).*

FIG 4.21: *A Greek Revival style detached house with a low pitched roof, which was distinctive of the Regency period. Note also the porch and pilasters which have Greek key decoration at the top under the eaves.*

FIG 4.23: *A house with a half basement and Greek Doric porch raised up a set of steps to make it more imposing.*

FIG 4.22: *Examples of Regency ironwork from balconies, which used patterns like scrolls, foliage, geometric and Greek key.*

piano nobile. Bay windows, which had been introduced in the second half of the 18th century, became popular especially in fashionable resorts, but unlike the earlier canted (angled) and semi-circular types, the Regency is notable for shallow bow windows usually the full height of the façade.

Many of these flamboyant styles persisted into the early Victorian period with classical terraces still dominant in the town and a new Italianate style popular on suburban villas, before the more serious and sombre red brick Gothic began to dominate (see *The Victorian House Explained* in this series).

FIG 4.24: *Regency doorways often had distinctive reeded, plain or patterned surrounds, which carried on over the arch of the fanlight as in this example.*

FIG 4.25: *An early 19th century window with thinner glazing bars and in this example a blind box at the top in which was originally stored a pull-out external blind to cast shade on the room within.*

FIG 4.26: *Early examples of bow windows on a hotel dating from the late 1770s. Later examples had larger expanses of glass with thinner glazing bars.*

FIG 4.27: *Chinese styles were fashionable in the Regency period, although this was mostly in interior design and furniture. The pagoda inspired design of balcony roofs, however, was a common and distinctive feature on the exterior of many Regency houses.*

Period Details

FIG 4.28: DOORS: *The front door to a house was typically a six panelled design (as opposed to the Victorian four panel) with a short top section, large middle and small to medium bottom. There was more variety in the Regency period with different shaped and deeper panels. These were usually fielded (with a raised central part and sunken bevelled edges) but in areas that were prone to dirt or damage might have a stronger flush panel with just a beaded edge (2, 3 and 17). Cheaper housing and doors out of sight on larger houses could use a simple plank and batten type (18). Early door surrounds could be flamboyant (19), some still with Baroque style hoods (1 and 15), or more usually a flat top supported on brackets originally without a fanlight at this date (3 and 14). Later entrances might have no surround due to taste and building regulations and the decoration was put into the fanlight (7 and 9) while some finer houses had classical stone pedimented pieces (2, 11, 12, 20 and 24). There was a wider range of styles in the late 18th century and into the Regency period, such as Gothick (21); while some were extravagant (6 and 8), others were restrained with the moulding going up the sides and continuing over the arch or square top (16 and 23). Doors could be painted in a white lead paint, black or dark green.*

FIG 4.29: FANLIGHTS: *Fanlights became popular from the mid 18th century to illuminate the narrow hall behind the front door. They may have also been fitted to existing as well as new houses with the old doors shortened (the middle or upper panels are often reduced in height) or replaced to accommodate a rectangular shape opening. Early types tend to have thicker wooden or metal bars, and more simple designs by the mid 18th century, taking the form of an arch with fanned segments. Later styles from the 1770s became more delicate (5, 14 and 21), sometimes very elaborate (22 and 25) and occasionally with Gothick style tracery (7 and 27). Most were semi-circular in shape with a batwing (1, 5 and 16) being a popular pattern. Improved metal working techniques through the Napoleonic wars allowed decorative fanlights to be cheaper until new sheet glass in the 1830s made the intricate glazing bars obsolete and Victorian types tend to be rectangular with only a few geometric bars, if any.*

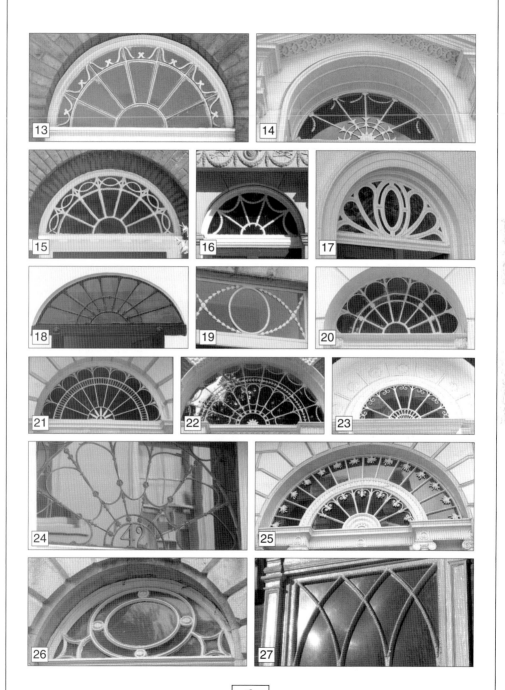

FIG 4.30: SASH WINDOWS: *Vertically sliding sash windows dominated houses throughout the period, either with both sashes moving over each other supported by pulleys and weights or, in cheaper examples, simply held open by wedges. A notable change in design was the position of the sash box or frame within the wall, at first exposed and flush (4 and 8) then later set back (7) and after the 1774 Building Act hidden behind the brickwork or masonry (10 and 12). The other improvement was the thickness of the glazing bars –thicker at first (2, 8 and 11) but gradually thinning and with the insertion of metal into them in the Regency period they became very fine, coupled with new larger sheets of glass (9 and 10). The twelve pane window was the most common, its proportions suiting the classical style terrace although sixteen pane types (3, 6, 8 and 11) were also common. Some sash windows had sidelights to make a triple set (5) or had semi-circular heads (12).*

FIG 4.31: OTHER WINDOWS: *There was also a wide range of distinctive window shapes, most with sashes but some still with casement openings (side hinged) (12). Venetian windows (with a tall semi-circular opening and two square headed sidelights) were used by Palladian designers and remained popular throughout the century (1, 6, 9 and 15). Semi-circular shapes were also common, often used in conjunction with Venetians (7 and 9), and round or elliptical windows were used, too, especially early on in the period (5). Dormer windows set in the roof to illuminate the attic were prominent in the early decades (13) but were hidden behind the parapet in Palladian style terraces and most later examples. Bay windows came into fashion after being introduced by Robert Taylor in the 1750s and 60s. The earlier ones tend to be canted (angled sides) (8), then curved in the later 18th century (16), with the bowed, elliptical type popular in the Regency period (11). On cheaper housing or on the upper floor under the eaves of larger houses, a shorter, horizontally sliding sash window that did not need pulleys was used (2, 4 and 18) – commonly known as Yorkshire sashes. In the top storey workshops of mill town terraces longer versions of these were used (14, 20, 21 and 22).*

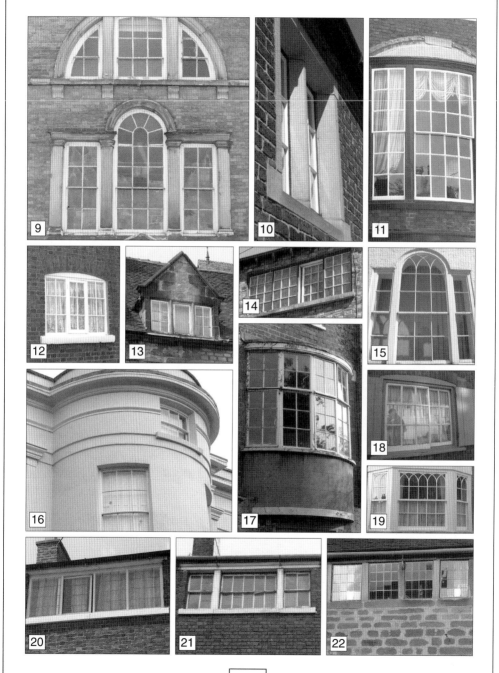

FIG 4.32: WINDOW DETAILS: *Most windows through the period had no decorative surrounds but on finer houses, especially stone and earlier examples, raised classical mouldings around the edges were used (8), often with a pedimented top to emphasis the centre or the piano nobile (6). Later Gothick style houses also used a drip mould above the window (11). Security from rioting and theft was a problem for many as was protection from the elements so external window shutters were fitted, often just on the ground floor but in some cases on all windows (1, 2 and 13). They were held on simple pin hinges (4) and kept back against the wall by stays (3, 5 and 12) when open but were locked from the inside when shut by bolts (1 and 13). Protection from the sun was also required for residents, furniture, carpets and fabrics so external pull-down blinds became popular in the Regency period to shade the windows and even doors (see Fig 4.28.23). When not in use they withdrew up behind a blind box or pelmet, which usually had a simple decorative profile, and it is these that often remain on houses (7, 8, 9 and 10).*

FIG 4.33: RAINWATER TRAPS AND PIPES: *On most early and some later Georgian houses the water that ran off the roof came through gaps in the parapet and was collected in wooden guttering lined with lead, which has long since perished. Later examples were in cast iron with a metal trap at the front; these were usually decorated, sometimes with elaborate patterns (6, 9 and 10) and frequently with a date (1, 3, 8, 11, 12, 13 and 14) – although this may be of a revision to the house and not its original date of construction. The iron pipes that channelled the water down to the ground were held to the wall by flat straps (3, 4 and 9), which could be shaped (15) or decorated (5, 7 and 14).*

11

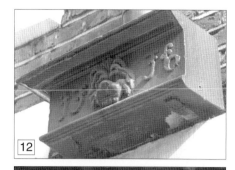

12

13

15

14

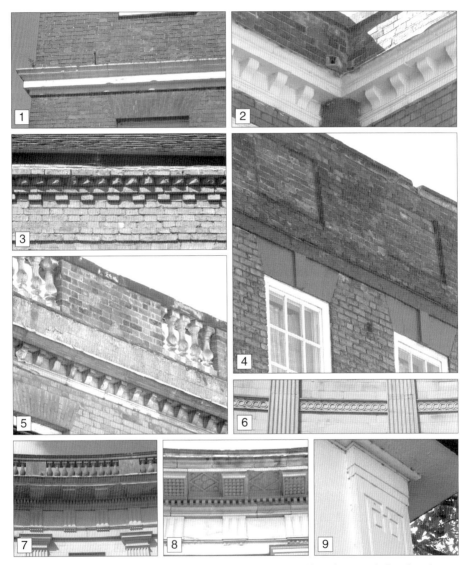

FIG 4.34: EXTERIOR DECORATION: *The exterior wall surface tended to be plain on many Georgian houses but some decoration or raised features were permitted, such as the cornice (1, 2, 3, 5, 13 and 14), string course (16), decorative bands and pilasters (6, 9 and 11), quoins (15) and the parapet at the top (4, 5, 7, 10 and 12). Early examples could be elaborate, especially the cornice (14), while later decoration tends to have shallow mouldings (9 and 11).*

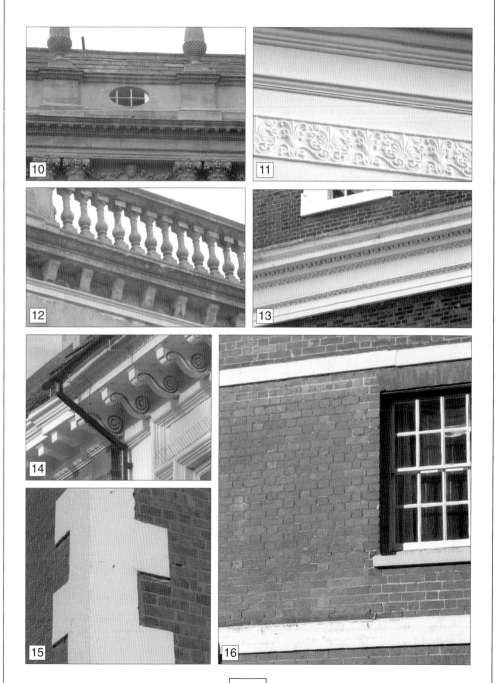

10

11

12

13

14

15

16

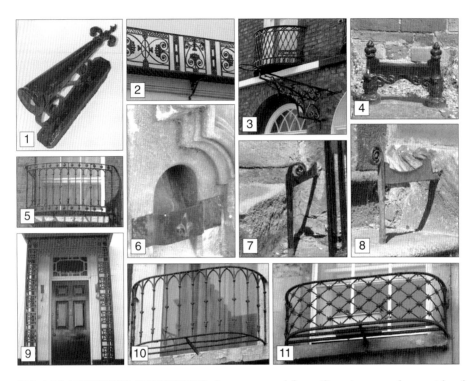

FIG 4.35: EXTERIOR IRONWORK: *Iron was used for utility pieces on the outside of the house throughout the period. Foot-scrapers were essential as there were few paved surfaces and the roads could be full of mud and muck. They could be fairly plain (7, 8 and 23), decorative (4, 13, 19 and 24) or set within a recess in the wall (6, 18 and 22). The naked flame used for lighting had to be extinguished by pushing it into a snuffer, an upside down iron cone on the outside of the house (1, 14, 17 and 20). A lantern was often fitted above the steps leading to the door, usually supported on an iron arch or brackets, of which original examples often survive although the lanterns are later replacements (3, 16, 17 and 20). Decorative ironwork came into its own in the Regency period, especially by the 1820s when mass produced, cast iron decorative pieces could be ordered from catalogues. Wrought and cast iron window guards (3, 5, 10, 11 and 21), balconies supported on brackets cantilevered off the main wall by iron beams set back into the house (2, 12 and 15) and porches (9) date from the late 18th century when simple diagonal patterns came into fashion to the more elaborate and common Regency types. Door furniture was limited to a door knocker and knob and was usually made from cast iron and painted black, although later replacements (as most seen these days are) are often brass (25 and 26). Lion's heads, urns and simple rings were popular shapes for the knocker.*

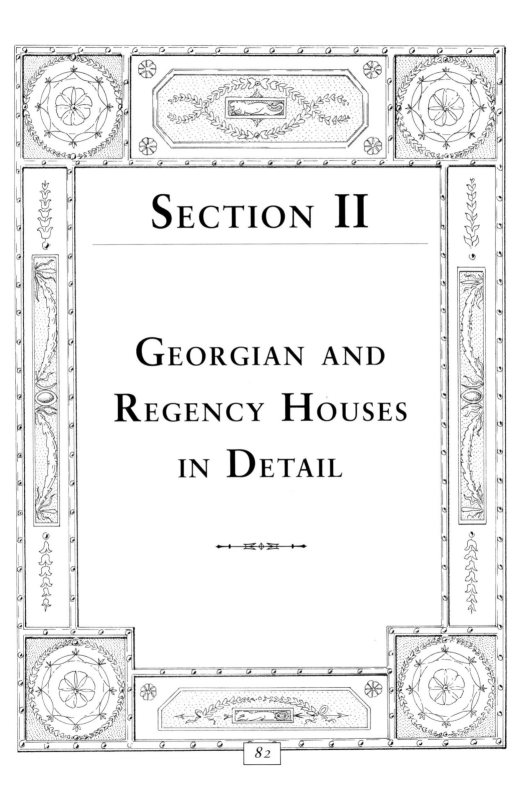

SECTION II

GEORGIAN AND REGENCY HOUSES IN DETAIL

CHAPTER 5

General Fittings and Decoration

FIG 5.1: *An interior view, with labels of some of the fittings and parts of the wall.*

The interiors of Georgian and Regency houses were, in their largest and finest examples, a showcase of classical taste intended to impress the increasing number of guests. Improved transport and the development of the Season in large towns and cities encouraged a vibrant social life and even those of a modest income tried to emulate the lifestyle and houses of the rich. Yet the wealth enjoyed by the aristocracy was not spread wide; the new middle classes were still small in number and yet to find their own voice and the majority of the population spent their irregular and unreliable income on living, most having little in the way of possessions and no time or money for decorating.

For the well-off whose large and medium sized houses are the focus of this book, there was an ever changing range of styles to shape the interior, and more professional architects, designers, craftsmen and decorators armed with new pattern books and first-hand experience of classical architecture to carry out the work. At the beginning of the period, Baroque, with its fanciful shapes and opulent decoration, was still in fashion (the name Baroque was coined as an insult directed at the previous style by the next generation of architects and means a misshaped pearl). This was replaced by the more refined and restrained Palladian, although interiors could still be flamboyant, before a final flowering of Baroque in the form of the lighter and more naturalistic Rococo style (named after the rocky incrustations that featured on the fashionable grottos of the time).

The second half of the 18th century was dominated by discoveries from Ancient Greek, Roman and Etruscan buildings and their reinterpretation by Robert Adam in particular. Interior moulding becomes shallow, lighter and delicate, space is used to better effect

FIG 5.2: *A restored Rococo ceiling with a white background and gilded mouldings from Great Witley church, Worcestershire.*

with niches and colonnaded alcoves, and surfaces are decorated with swags, vases and husks highlighted in gold. Finally, in the Regency period the Neo Classical and Greek Revival of the past generation is further influenced by Chinese, Egyptian, French and Gothick styles to create a wide range of geometric, naturalistic, classical and historic forms. Later in the period the mixing of different elements in a single scheme also become acceptable, an eclectic mix that was to be distinctive of early Victorian interiors.

The owner not only had to be aware of the latest fashions and design etiquette but also where to focus most of his efforts. As the intention was to impress well-to-do guests it was the reception rooms that received the most lavish decoration, with the family rooms and bedrooms, which were out of sight, having a lower status of furnishing. This hierarchy of decoration, with the principal rooms on the piano nobile at the top and the servants' quarters at the bottom, is important when considering the past use of rooms within a house – where if original fittings remain, such as fireplaces and decorative mouldings, the best should be found in the former and the latter will be devoid of most. Even in the details, money could be saved by simplifying the style of staircase once it was past the first floor rooms or by giving doors lavish moulding and fielded panels on the side facing the public while the other, which was viewed only by the family or staff, could be plain.

Another aspect of the 18th century house was accommodation for the servants. Most large urban houses would, like their rural counterparts, have a wide range of specialist staff from the butler, housekeeper and cook at the top to the scullery maid at the bottom. Even modest middle class households would expect to have a number of staff including a maid of all work, which in the smaller home could be a lonely job entailing a working day of at least fifteen hours! Female staff were a recent development; in the past, men waited on the rich, with a housekeeper and maids only becoming common in the late 17th century. The position of staff within the house was also changing from being part of the household, living and sleeping alongside their lord in a medieval home, to the strictly segregated and regulated positions within a Victorian house. For instance, at the beginning of the period, servants would use the main stairs along with the family, yet by Regency times separate sets of stairs, often in a rear extension, permitted them to go about their work out of sight.

The principal positions within the urban house were those of the butler, who presided over the dining room and was responsible for the wine cellar and the silver, and the housekeeper, who kept a close eye on the storeroom and household accounts and served tea in the drawing room. The cook ran the kitchen, while footmen had diverse jobs, which included serving at the table, answering the front door, manning the carriage and announcing their arrival when travelling with the family. These servants and the rooms required to carry out their jobs grew in number through the period, affecting the layout of the already tightly packed terrace house.

FIG 5.3: *A late 18th century fireplace surround designed by Robert Adam with female figurines (caryatids) supporting the mantel and a central plaque with a raised decorative scene.*

Fireplaces

The most important feature in a room for both function and display was the fireplace. Not only was it the source of heat, but its surround gave ample opportunity for decoration, making it the focal point of the room. In most, it was positioned against a party wall, one in the front room and another in the rear, but in some early examples it was fitted in the corner where the central dividing wall met the party wall.

GRATES

The centre of the fireplace was the cast iron grate in which the fuel was held within the hearth. Wood had been the most widely used fuel in the past, although coal had its place in areas where it could be easily dug out, or it was imported when there was not much wood (coal from Newcastle was shipped down to London from an early date). In the 18th century, however, coal was growing in popularity,

FIG 5.4: *Examples of 18th century basket grates with small holders for the coal, which burns better in a compact mass than in the larger types used for wood.*

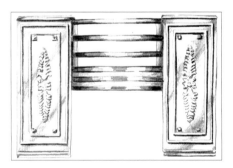

FIG 5.5: *Examples of hob grates, the left hand type dating from the late 18th century and the right from the early 19th. The hobs are on the solid parts to the side of the basket and allowed pots or kettles to be heated upon their tops.*

FIG 5.6: *Early register grates, the left hand example dating from the late 18th century and the right hand from the late Regency period. They were supplied as one piece in cast iron with the hinged register at the top behind the decorative surround. The whole grate was inserted within the fire surround.*

especially in the second half when improvements in canal, river and road travel made it cheaper and available in areas where it had not been before. The grate and the flue above were not drastically redesigned to make the most efficient use of coal and generally were simple baskets, which, as it burns better in a compact mass, were smaller than those used for wood. An early development was the hob grate, which made use of the heat given off laterally by fitting two rectangular blocks either side of the fire for heating and cooking upon its upper surface.

By the late 18th century attempts were being made to create more efficient grates and avoid the great loss of heat up the chimney and the draughts that were created around the room. In 1797 an American, Benjamin Rumford, suggested certain improvements to reflect more heat into the room and improve the flow of air into the fire. These included narrowing the throat of the flue and reducing the size of the fireplace, lowering the basket, bringing it forward, and angling the sides. However, we were slow to accept these new ideas and it was not until the

Victorian period that they became standard practice.

A development that did appear in the mid 18th century was the fitting of an adjustable damper called a register at

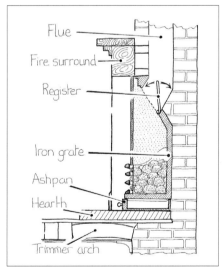

FIG 5.7: *A section through a fireplace showing the hinged register, which controlled the draw up the chimney. Due to the weight of the grate and surround a trimmer arch or beam might be fitted beneath the floorboards for support.*

the entrance to the flue, in order to control the draw of the fire. They slowly caught on and by the end of the Regency period were beginning to be cast in one piece along with the grate, sides and rear.

FIREPLACE SURROUNDS

Fireplace surrounds were the principal permanent decorative feature in a room and reflected the fashionable style of the time. They could be made from stone and marble, or from cheaper materials and painted to imitate them. Hardwoods were another choice for the finest rooms but the cheaper softwoods like pine were used in most and then stained or grained to look superior. The fireplace surround also reflects the hierarchy of decoration within the house, with the main reception rooms likely to have the finest examples and lesser rooms

upstairs the most simple and cheapest types (if any at all).

Many early fireplaces still retained bolection moulding, which had been popular since the late 17th century, around the three sides of the opening, while elaborate Baroque style surrounds were still acceptable even within some new Palladian houses. The new classical style surrounds that came into fashion often featured bold Roman decoration and 'earing' at the top of the jambs (where the moulding steps out like ears). Mid century styles included Rococo with its naturalistic decoration and curving opening and then a little later the Adam style fireplace with a smaller overall size, more restrained detailing from Greek and Roman sources and a central plaque.

Later Georgian and Regency period surrounds tend to retain Adam's restrained mouldings and refined detailing with new styles like the Gothick adding variety to the decoration. The most characteristic form of surround at the time was to

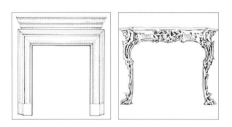

FIG 5.8: *Examples of early fireplace surrounds. The left hand example from the 1720s has a bolection moulding around three sides of the opening, as had been in fashion since the late 17th century. The right hand example is in a Rococo style and dates from the mid 18th century. Mantels are small at this date as it was not fashionable to put ornaments upon them.*

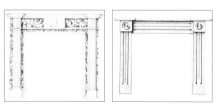

FIG 5.9: *Examples of later fireplace surrounds. The left hand example is in a Neo Classical style with fluted pilasters, marble inserts and a central decorative plaque. The right hand surround has the classic Regency form of fluted jambs and lintel and bull's-eyes in the corners.*

have bull's-eyes in the corners and reeding up the sides (jambs) and sometimes along the top. The mantelpiece on most Georgian surrounds was narrow, only stepping out above the brackets and columns up the vertical sides, but with more artefacts to display in many principal rooms a deeper mantel shelf developed in the later Regency period (although deep mantels are often one way of identifying Victorian fireplaces, they also could be fitted at a later date to Georgian ones).

FLUES AND CHIMNEYS

As with the grate, there had been little development in the design of the flue and chimney above. The flue openings were large enough for chimney sweeps' climbing boys to be sent up to clean them (see Chapter 1). This practice was banned in 1829 but by then the size of flue was being reduced to around nine inches to improve the draw and would have been too thin for boys to access anyway. The flues and chimney were usually made from brick, even in stone houses, (although the chimney at the top would have been of stone or stone-faced) and were generally shaped like a tuning fork, with the flues from the fireplaces in the front room running up one arm and those from the back up the other, meeting together at the top as they emerged outside within the chimney. The number of pots or openings on the chimney generally indicates the number of fires there would have originally been but it is important to note that many bedrooms may not have had a fireplace at all, and those

that did were often only lit when someone was ill.

Chimneys were generally plain in style until some extravagantly decorated pieces became popular on Gothick and exotic styled houses in the Regency period. Chimney pots were not originally fitted to Georgian houses; they were only introduced in the early 19th century to improve the draw and later put on top of older stacks.

Stairs

The stairs were usually positioned centrally within a classically designed detached house and to the side in a terrace, in both cases by this period usually accessed via the hall and positioned at the rear of the building (in some earlier and most working class houses the front door opened directly into the main front room). The balustrades and newel posts gave opportunity for owners to impress their guests, but on the upper floors, out of sight of visitors, the same parts would usually be of a simple design to save costs.

Early types of stairs from the 17th century were wooden structures supported by newel posts, which in part directed the weight down onto the floor upon which they rested. However, by the Georgian period the open string stair, with the balustrades resting directly upon the treads, which in turn were cantilevered out of the wall, made for graceful ascents that seem to float in the air. Balustrades were usually paired upon a tread early on and later set in threes with various turned patterns such as the barley twist, which was

FIG 5.10: *Examples of open string staircases where the balusters sit upon the top of the treads with decorated exposed sides. The barley twist balusters in the top example were popular in the mid 18th century and the iron types in the bottom date from the Regency period.*

popular in the first half of the 18th century. Later in the period plain wooden and, in the finest houses, iron balustrades were fashionable with polished dark wood handrails finishing at the bottom in a spiral being a hallmark of Regency houses. Another feature of some of the large houses in this latter period was to illuminate the top of the staircase with a skylight.

Interior Doors

The six panelled door was the standard design for most internal doors. This was not just due to classical taste; the shortage of large pieces of timber during this period meant that these framed panelled types, which used less wood than an old fashioned stout plank and batten door, made economic sense. Those examples that opened onto the reception rooms would have been the finest in hardwoods (such as mahogany) or a softwood (pine and fir were popular) grained to look like them or just flat painted. They would have

FIG 5.11: *Details from Regency staircases with plain or decorated iron balusters, hardwood handrails and spiral ends on the ground floor.*

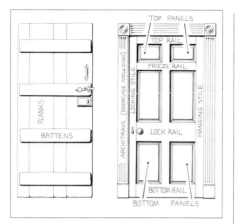

FIG 5.12: *A plank and batten door (left) from this date would tend to have horizontal battens holding planks, which could vary in width (later Victorian types have regular width planks and extra diagonal battens). These were found in attics and service rooms in larger buildings and in basic urban and rural housing. The six panelled door (right) is the classic Georgian and Regency design (before the four panelled door became standard in the Victorian period).*

had fielded panels although the depth of these does not tend to be as deep as on later Victorian types. Lesser rooms would have had simpler designs and it is possible to find doors with a fielded panel facing out to guests and a plainer reverse side where they were only seen by the family or servants. Simple plank and batten doors may have sufficed for service rooms and servants' accommodation in the attic.

Door furniture was generally simple with lever handles popular in the early 18th century and round or oval knobs for the rest of the period, either in iron or brass. Some of the finest may have had a decorated metal escutcheon plate behind the knob, others from the late 18th century had brass finger plates above it where the hand was likely to come in contact with the door. Locks became increasingly popular as households looked for more privacy. Most at this date were surface mounted rim locks in iron or brass casings but by the early 19th century mortice locks set within the door came into fashion with

FIG 5.13: *Examples of the door furniture.*

a small metal escutcheon covering the keyhole.

Ceilings and Floors

Plaster ceilings were relatively new at the beginning of the Georgian period. Timber framed houses usually had the underside of the joists supporting the upper floor open on view and in the best cases decorated. It was only with the influence of classical style in the late 16th century in the best houses and during the 17th century for most others that a plastered ceiling fixed to the underside of the joists became common. Laths, thin strips of wood, were nailed at right angles to the underside of the joists and the plaster built up in layers upon them with the first coat pushed hard up between the laths to make a good fixing.

In most houses the finished surface was left plain and painted white, with any decoration in the cornice around the edge. In the best houses plaster mouldings were applied, with earlier types having deeper mouldings and later shallower. Adam style ceilings, which continued to be popular throughout the second half of this period, had delicate mouldings with a central round or oval piece and panels or bands around the edge, many of which were applied ready-made from sheets of canvas or paper. Some of the finest ceilings were painted with classical scenes; Regency ones could be very heavy and simple in design, while others were decorated to appear as a blue sky with clouds. Ceiling roses, which were fitted for decoration and to collect soot rising from the oil lamp or candles below, were really a Victorian feature although they did appear in some Regency houses.

Solid floors in the basement and the ground level of some houses could be covered in marble or stone in the finest situation, or brick, quarry tile or just beaten earth covered in straw in service areas and basic urban and rural housing. Most floors were boarded,

FIG 5.14: *A ceiling from a ruined house showing the laths fixed to the joists and the plaster coated on top.*

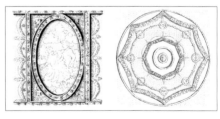

FIG 5.15: *Decorated plaster ceilings from large houses. The example on the left dates from the early 18th century and has deep moulding while the one to the right is an Adam style example and has shallow, delicate details.*

with planks of oak in the early and best houses and pine or fir in most others, often supplied from the Baltic as good timber here became scarce. Early Georgian boards tend to be wider but later on thinner pieces around 5–8 inches were used in the best houses as they distorted less, with planks 8–10 inches used elsewhere. Most were hand-cut boards and not always of regular size, butted up against each other and nailed through on top of each end. In the finest examples the nails were hit in at an angle into the cut edge which was then covered when the next board was butted up to it, hence hiding the nail head. Tongue and groove was occasionally used but machine cut boards were not widespread until the late 19th century. Again, if softwood was used, it was usually treated to simulate a better quality wood as a sizable part of the floor was left exposed.

Wall to wall carpets were a luxury that became fashionable for a while in the late 18th century and most were made in thin strips a couple of feet wide and cut and sewn together on site to fit the room. Others had a large carpet piece or rug in the centre of the room with the boards exposed around the edge. This was easier in the days before vacuum cleaners as it could be removed outside, although most carpet cleaning was done by servants on their hands and knees with dustpan and brush. A cheaper option was to use woven rush matting or floorcloths, the latter being canvas or cloth stiffened with linseed oil or layers of pigment and then painted with a pattern or an imitation of a better quality floor. They were used along halls and corridors and in lesser rooms like bedrooms and dressing rooms.

Walls

STRUCTURE

The interior surface of brick, stone and internal timber framed walls was either panelled or plastered. The former was the traditional method, which was still to be found in the early part of the period, with the old square framed panelling being replaced by classically proportioned pieces above and below the chair rail (see Fig 6.1). Plastering a wall had become popular in the late 17th century as it reduced the fire risk and most walls in late Georgian and Regency homes would have been finished this way (panelling remained in some later houses below the chair

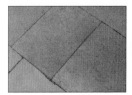

FIG 5.16: *Examples of stone, quarry tile and floorboards from Georgian and Regency houses.*

FIG 5.17: *Examples of walls showing the plaster applied in layers, with the first two scored or pitted to give grip to the next coat. Some have been applied onto laths pinned on the brickwork, others were put directly onto the wall. These are from the ruined houses at Witley Court, Worcestershire and Sutton Scarsdale Hall, Nottinghamshire and are worth visiting if you wish to understand the structure of 18th century houses.*

rail especially in the drawing room).

The plaster layers could be applied directly to the brick or masonry or onto thin laths nailed to the wall. The plaster was made from crushed limestone, heated to produce quick lime, and then mixed with water and left for a number of weeks to produce lime putty. This was then mixed with sand and water before being applied to the wall in three gradually thinner coats (animal hair was often put into the first coats for strength). The finished surfaces of the first two were scored to increase the grip of the next coat and each one had to be left to dry for another few weeks before the next could be applied.

MOULDINGS: DADO, CORNICE, PICTURE RAIL AND SKIRTING

The finished wall and ceiling were broken up and decorated by a series of elaborate mouldings in the more important rooms and fewer and plainer ones elsewhere. The cornice (or coving in its plain concave form) covered up the joint between the ceiling and the wall and was usually made from plaster or wood, with a series of shaped grooves and projections from classical forms (see Fig 5.18), or a repeating pattern often with an egg and dart or dentil feature along the bottom edge. Regency types tend to be simpler.

The dado or chair rail was usually made from wood as its purpose was to protect the wall from the backs of chairs, which were stored or grouped around the edge of rooms in the first part of the period. It too was moulded from a series of classical forms and later with a reeded form in the Regency

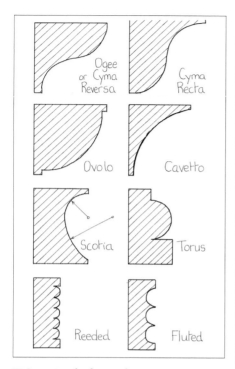

FIG 5.19: *Examples of panelling (top three), cornice (bottom left), door architrave (bottom centre) and skirting (bottom right) from Georgian and Regency houses.*

FIG 5.18: *The basic elements used to make up mouldings used in Georgian and Regency houses.*

period. As the table became a permanent feature in the centre of dining rooms and the chairs moved with it, the dado rail fell from favour and the picture rail a foot or so below the cornice, from which framed artwork could be hung, became popular.

The skirting covered the gap between the wall and the floor and protected the wall in this vulnerable position. They tended to be simple in design with just a concave or ogee shaped moulding and a single beading along the top edge. They were usually a dark colour, brown

was popular and practical, especially in the Regency period.

DECORATION

The walls could be finished in a number of ways. Painting was done on the plastered surface using distemper, a traditional recipe of chalk and pigment mixed with water and bound together with animal glue (in this period it was only oil bound types used on wood and metal work that were referred to as paint). Georgian walls were coloured with pastel shade paints, especially stone colours, greys, greens and pinks, although stronger colours were used in dining rooms and to highlight decorative details (for instance, gilded details on a light green background, which was popular in Adam's interiors). In the late Georgian and Regency period stronger colours became more available and popular, especially after 1820, with rich orange reds and crimson as a background to set off the gilt framed pictures becoming fashionable in male rooms.

FIG 5.20: *Wallpaper patterns could range from the elaborate classical arrangements with vases and husks (left), Chinese designs with simple stylised birds and foliage (middle) and in the Regency period strong striped patterns (right), in this case with anthemion motifs, a popular form from this date.*

The alternative to paints was hangings of fabric, which were stretched over battens. Wallpaper was at the time still hand-made and supplied in short sheets, making it very expensive and rare until machine-made mass production in the early 19th century allowed it to become fashionable in late Regency and Victorian homes. Where used in the finest houses, both of these types reflected the fashionable décor of the day, with Chinese patterns, classical designs and floral arrangements popular in the later 18th century, and stripes in the Regency period.

Windows

Most early glass was hand-made crown glass, which was blown and spun on a metal rod to produce a disc from which the small rectangles of glass were cut. This leaves an attractive distortion (curved and rippled), a slight green or blue tinge and tiny air bubbles, which distinguish original glass from the later smooth product. The bull's-eye where the rod made contact with the glass,

which is often a feature of period style windows today, was never used on Georgian houses and was usually thrown back in the furnace. Cylinder glass (where a long vessel is produced at the end of the rod and then cut open to produce a flat sheet) meant that larger panes could be produced although not of the same quality. Plate glass had been around since the 17th century but production of flat sheets, being very labour intensive and expensive, was mainly used for mirrors in Georgian houses. New methods of production of plate glass made it more widely available from the 1830s and resulted in Victorian windows having fewer glazing bars if any (due to this a small projection in the bottom corner of the upper sash, called a horn, was

FIG 5.21: *Details from internal shutters showing how they were locked in place by a central bar when closed.*

built in to give strength to the joint and is a way of telling later windows even if they do have glazing bars).

Internal hinged shutters were usually fitted on the sides of windows, especially after the middle of the 18th century. They were stored in recesses on each side and hinged open with two or three shutters to cover the window, mainly to protect the precious furniture and fabrics from fading but also to provide privacy and extra security. Some later types could be stored below the window and pulled up. There would also be a series of coverings in the finest rooms, from outer curtains to lighter fabrics behind and, in some cases, pull-down blinds nearest to the window.

Lighting

The Georgian and Regency house at night would have appeared a very dim place, with small splashes of light and glowing embers from the fire. Most light sources were portable and could be carried around from room to room, so, for instance, there would not usually be a permanent light in the bedroom – the occupants would take candles up to bed with them.

Candles provided most light, ranging from cheap rush dips – these were no more than common rushes dipped in animal fat, producing a dim glow, a lot of soot and only lasting an hour at best – up to beeswax candles, which were very expensive and used only for special occasions, even by the well off. Dips were simply clipped into holders while tallow and beeswax candles were held in candlesticks, wall sconces (with mirrors behind to reflect the light) and, in the best houses, chandeliers.

Oil lamps were better although expensive but they became more popular as they were improved upon in the late 18th century. This was done by increasing the air flow to the flame so that it gave off more light and less smoke, and by raising the oil reservoir above the light to use gravity to enhance the flow of oil to the wick. Rape seed, olive or palm oil were typically used (the Victorians preferred paraffin oil, which being thinner meant the reservoir no longer needed to be held above the flame and later ones from this period have it below).

Although the first gas supplies were being laid on in the Regency period, at this date it was usually used in industry and street lighting; it was not until gaslights were installed in the new Houses of Parliament that they became popular in the home from the 1850s.

CHAPTER 6

Reception and Family Rooms

FIG 6.1: *The drawing room was one of the principal reception rooms in which owners would display their wealth or taste, with lavish decoration. In this example, panelling on the walls (still in favour until the late 18th century), decorated plaster ceiling and a rich carpet would impress upon guests the standing of their host.*

Large and medium houses

The role of the main rooms in Georgian and Regency houses was changing throughout the period. The open plan medieval hall had evolved into a number of principal rooms, with a general but not specific designation; flexible furniture, which could be pulled out and pushed back

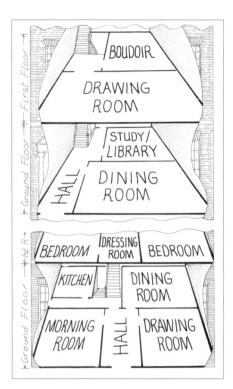

FIG 6.3: *A view of a dining room as it may have looked in the late 18th century. It was a luxuriously fitted out room in the finest houses, with a marbled fireplace, decorative plaster ceiling, mahogany furniture and strongly coloured walls to best show off the gilt framed pictures.*

FIG 6.2: *A cut away showing one type of arrangement of rooms on the ground and first floor of a terraced house (top) and a detached house (bottom).*

against the wall when not in use, reflected this multi-purpose nature. During the 18th century there is a gradual move away from this flexibility and rooms become more numerous and for specific uses, with more permanent furniture and fixings. This trend is most notable in the dining room.

DINING ROOM
In large and medium sized houses the dining room was mainly used for entertaining guests and special occasions; a separate morning or breakfast room, or a front kitchen or parlour in smaller houses, would have been used at other times. In terraced houses it could usually be found at the front on the piano nobile or sometimes below on the ground floor and, as it was mainly used by the gentlemen after dinner, it had a very masculine feel to the furniture and decoration.

Early dining rooms still retained flexibility, with the main table removable along with the chairs to the side of the room when the meal was complete. However, by the late 18th century, it was fashionable for a large table to be positioned permanently in the centre so the chair or dado rail was removed and a picture rail fitted from which gentlemen could hang artwork for the admiration of their fellows. The room also gained height, being about a foot taller by the Regency years than at the opening of the Georgian period, usually with a chandelier hanging from the centre of the ceiling in the finest houses. Dark or bold colours were often used on the walls to offset the gilt frames, with a sea green and later crimson red being popular although lighter schemes were also used. There would have been a sideboard from which the butler could serve the food and wine, a cabinet for the diners to help themselves to drinks after the meal when servants were banished, and card or games tables for gambling.

The times and arrangements of meals for the wealthy were different in the Georgian and Regency periods. Dinner was taken in the afternoon between 2 pm and 5 pm in the earlier part of this era, changing to a time that we ourselves would be more comfortable with – around 5 pm to 7 pm – by the early 19th century (most people away from the fashionable centres would have a main meal in the middle of the day). Dinner could begin with a starter and then two main courses followed; the first might include fish, ham, mutton or chicken, the second game, pies, tarts and vegetables (the latter were not popular early in the period as they were believed to be bad for you!). Desserts, including fruits, sugar, marzipan and even liquorice would end the meal.

When finished, the ladies would leave the room and the gentlemen would entertain themselves and drink, usually excessively. Without the convenience of inside toilets in most houses, the inevitable relieving of themselves was done within a pot passed around under the table or in a corner and stored within a sideboard or cupboard!

DRAWING ROOM

While the so called 'gentlemen' became steadily inebriated, the ladies retired to the drawing room, a more peaceful, feminine room where they would be served tea. This was a popular drink at the time but still expensive and was served weak and without milk in the style of the Orient. Tealeaves were kept under lock and key and when finished with were passed on to the servants to be used again or to be sold locally.

The drawing room (derived from the earlier 'withdrawing room') was situated on the piano nobile in terraced houses and was either adjacent to the dining room or above it; in the latter case there would be a second similar room behind or a main bedroom in medium sized houses. It was a more flexible space than the dining room, being the place where guests were entertained by the family or shown into for sherry before a meal, and where ladies returned afterwards to admire artwork, play cards or for conversation. In medium sized houses it could also be used by the ladies for painting, crafts and reading and, in some later examples, even taking breakfast.

The furniture, as a result, was more flexible. Early in the period chairs and tables were set around the perimeter of the room with the centre being open but by Regency times a more relaxed

FIG 6.4: *The drawing room was the other principal reception room into which guests were shown before a meal and where the ladies retired afterwards. In this example it is a lighter, more feminine space, reflecting this use. The dado rail, which had fallen from favour in the dining room, was still fitted here as chairs continued to be rested up against the wall.*

FAMILY ROOMS

In large and medium sized houses there would be other rooms for the use of the family, generally on the ground floor. A morning or breakfast room was provided in larger houses, while the drawing room was reserved for guests and family leisure pursuits, and breakfast could be taken here. They tended to be light, airy rooms at the front of the house and had similar arrangements to the drawing room, although with less impressive decoration and fireplaces.

In some earlier and rural houses a general parlour (from the French verb *parler*, meaning 'to speak') was used for everyday meals and conversation. As it was not generally seen by guests the décor was less elaborate than in the reception rooms, with just a cornice or coving and skirting board and a fireplace with a cheaper but still reasonably decorative surround.

arrangement of the furniture, which would be set in small informal groups around the room, was fashionable. A dado rail, therefore, remained popular, to protect the walls. There would often be built-in bookcases and many of the largest had double doors opening to the other room on the piano nobile, to create a larger space when entertaining.

The décor of the room reflected its feminine nature, with generally lighter colours and more delicate and refined furnishings. Rose pink and, later, light greens were popular for the walls while in the Regency period there was a trend towards bringing the outside into the room, with full height sashes and later French windows and mirrors positioned to reflect the exterior foliage.

FIG 6.5: *The morning room was an informal family room in larger houses used for leisure, light meals, writing and reading. In this Regency example there is a table for breakfast, a writing desk and an upholstered armchair.*

The 18th century saw an increase in literacy which, coupled with an interest in the sciences and the ancient world, made the collecting of books a growing pastime. Previously a small closet off the bedchamber would have sufficed but now the wealthy gentleman needed a larger, specific room to house his books so a library or a study was often provided. In the more spacious terrace house it was found at the rear, with built-in bookcases (glass fronted early on, open later), writing desks, sometimes space for artwork and antiquities to be displayed and a lectern with an ancient manuscript or book of note upon it. Despite its masculine nature it could still be used by other members for letter writing, playing cards or for meeting guests.

HALL

The hall had fallen from being the impressive central room in medieval and Tudor houses to become a simple passage in most 18th century terraces. In the larger detached house it could still be a noteworthy space leading to the stairs at the rear, with a stone or marbled floor and family portraits on the walls – before they were relegated and replaced with classical artefacts, niches or columns in the finest later examples. In the terrace it was trapped at the side, making it a long, thin room with an arch at the end supporting the main dividing wall between the front and rear rooms and with the stairs beyond this. Walls were often painted in a common colour like stone to suit the hall's lower status and to comple-ment the rooms leading off it, the floor

FIG 6.6: PICKFORD'S HOUSE, FRIAR GATE, DERBY: *This hall from a large detached house is a wide central space with stone floor, decorative plaster ceiling and plain coloured walls so as to complement the principal reception rooms which lead from it.*

was either stone, marble or floor-boards, and lighting was limited to a simple pendant oil lamp and whatever daylight passed through the fanlight.

BEDROOMS

The bedrooms were positioned on the first floor and above, and their size and elaboration of décor gradually reduced the higher they went to reflect the status of the occupant, from the owner to the servants. In the finest houses the husband and wife might have separate sleeping quarters while in the smallest

FIG 6.7: *The bedroom in this Regency example has a four-poster bed with curtains to keep the draughts out, a dressing table, mirror, chest of drawers, wardrobe (with pull-out drawers rather than a hanging rail within) and a small table for taking light meals and tea. If there was no adjoining dressing room then a wash-stand would also have been in here and baths would have been taken in front of the fire in a metal tub.*

FIG 6.8: PICKFORD'S HOUSE: *An example of a four-poster bed. It was not designed just to be imposing but to support the curtains, which were drawn around it to keep out draughts. This was important as the room was rarely heated (there would have been a fire but it was only usually lit if someone was ill or at bath time).*

the whole family would have fitted into the one room.

The Georgian and Regency bedroom was not only for sleeping and dressing but also for washing as bathrooms were non-existent early on and rare even at the turn of the 19th century. This was partly because piped water, where laid on, was of too low a pressure to reach up to the first and second floor but also because when there were servants to bring it up and help you dress why would you need it anyway! Even when it was provided, later in the Victorian period, many of the upper classes did without a bathroom despite those below them on the social ladder having them fitted.

This meant that there would be a wash cabinet, usually set in a corner, with a marble top, wash-basin and jugs on top for everyday cleaning. A metal hip-bath, usually stored elsewhere, was positioned in front of the fire and filled with jugs of hot water brought up by servants from the range or a copper in the kitchen for the periodic bath times.

In the finest bedrooms four-poster beds were still to be found with drapes (heavier fabrics earlier in the period, lighter cottons, chintzes and linen later) hung around to reduce draughts in a room that was unheated (fires were only used to permit the circulation of fresh air up the chimney or to be lit when someone was ill). Curtains around the bed were seen as rather unhygienic later and were replaced in the 19th century by half-tester beds with solely decorative drapes hung over a frame at the head of the bed. Beds were of wood at this date – it wasn't until the Victorian period that metal framed versions became popular, with wooden slats or strapping beneath. There would be a number of mattresses stacked upon each other with straw in the bottom one and feathers or hair in the top.

Other furniture would include a dressing table (if there was not a separate dressing room) usually positioned between the two front windows to gain the best light, a chest of drawers, a wardrobe with trays or shelves rather than a rail, small tables and chairs or chaise-longue. A chamber pot would also be found here in many houses, which would be emptied out in the external privy every morning by the maid.

Servants' bedrooms were usually in the attics although some slept in basements in smaller houses. Although furniture was limited and would be cheap or hand-me-downs from the family's rooms, there would still be a bed with mattress, a chest of drawers, chair and a washing basin and jug. This room might, however, be shared by more than one member of staff.

DRESSING ROOMS, BOUDOIRS AND CLOSETS

In the largest houses there would usually be additional rooms separate from or leading off the main bedrooms. Dressing rooms for both men and

FIG 6.9: PICKFORD'S HOUSE: *An example of a wash-stand where servants would bring a jug of hot water for daily washing and shaving either in the bedroom or a separate dressing room.*

women were popular (the male version was known as a 'cabinet' earlier in the period), giving more space in the bedroom itself, and they are often found as a small room adjacent to a main bedroom or in the small extension at the rear that came into use in the Regency period. They would contain a wash-stand with facilities for washing and shaving and also the chamber pot.

Boudoirs became fashionable around this time (from the French word *bouder*, meaning 'to sulk') as a relaxing space where women could sew or read, either next to the bedroom or in the smaller room at the rear on the piano nobile.

The closet was originally named after

the close stool (basically a chamber pot covered by a closed top with a hole in it), which was stored in here or in the dressing room. By this period it had also become a male sanctuary and was more luxuriously fitted than its purpose might suggest, in medium sized houses it might also double up as a study. It was still usually a small room, either off a bedroom or dressing room and increasingly by the Regency period in the small rear extension.

Flushing toilets began to appear in the late 18th century in the finest houses, assuming mains water was laid on and drains were in place. Many were fitted on the ground or first floor extension as the water pressure would only reach this far, and the early systems tended not always to be effective so many stuck with chamber pots.

Smaller Houses

RURAL HOUSING

The large house in the village for the vicar or doctor would reflect the style and layout of similar structures in the towns but medium sized farmhouses could have a different arrangement. In many there was no hall and the front door opened directly into the front room, a large living room and kitchen all in one (the 'houseplace' in the north) although later the cooking might be transferred to a kitchen and scullery at the rear. A parlour or sitting room could also be found off this at the front of the house. Behind this there would be a scullery and, in many, a dairy reflecting the working nature of the house, with the stairs usually between

them at the rear although up the side in some. In some parts of the north and west the old arrangement of having the byre for livestock attached to the side of the house continued into this period.

Smaller cottages for agricultural workers would usually have a main living room and kitchen all in one at the front with a small pantry and scullery behind it. Upstairs there would be one or two bedrooms accessed by a small staircase or a ladder in the smallest examples.

SMALL URBAN EXAMPLES

Surprisingly, things could be better in this period for the working classes in the town compared with the city. The backs to backs and small terraces, which became the slums in the Victorian period, were at this date rented by the better class of worker. Still there would usually only be a living room and kitchen all in one in a back to back, with a scullery or wash-house in the room behind in larger terraces. Upstairs there would be just one or two bedrooms; if it was the latter the mother and father would use one, with any babies kept with them, while the other children would use the other.

A large section of the population, however, was crammed into older terraces with other families and might have just the one room in which to live, eat and sleep. These were desperately poor conditions, although the long hours and the fact that many men ate and drank away from the home after work probably helped families adapt to the limited space.

CHAPTER 7

Service Rooms

FIG 7.1: *A Georgian kitchen in the basement of a large terrace house. The fireplace contains an early metal range with adjustable sides to vary the width of the fire and a smoke jack above, which turned the spit in front of it. All kitchens would have had a substantial wooden table for the preparation of meals, and dressers to keep pots, pans, and everyday crockery.*

The service rooms were positioned either at the rear corner of detached houses with cellars beneath or in the basement, especially in large and medium sized terraced houses. Later in the period, rear extensions began to be built to house a scullery now that piped water was becoming available in towns and, as the pipes ran down the backs, the kitchen usually moved to the rear basement room to be close to it. It was not until well into the Victorian period that large rear extensions containing the kitchen

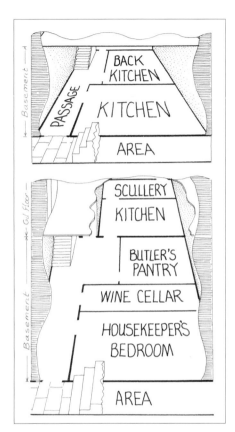

FIG 7.2: *Cut away views showing the possible arrangement of service rooms in a medium sized Georgian terrace (top) and a larger Regency house (bottom).*

FIG 7.3: PICKFORD'S HOUSE, FRIAR GATE, DERBY: *A restored kitchen with large fireplace and apparatus for roasting, cooking and boiling around a fire of adjustable width. There is also a central wooden table and a dresser along the back wall.*

and washrooms were built, providing staff with better working conditions, creating more privacy for the family and helping to keep cooking smells out of the house.

KITCHEN

The kitchen was the principal service room. It was where the cooking took place, although the washing and preparing of ingredients, the washing up afterwards and storage of food was usually done elsewhere in larger houses (there would rarely be a sink in the kitchen in this period). The focus of the room was the fireplace with a range set in the opening. Earlier in the period the range was always an open type with an adjustable basket to hold the coals and various jacks, cranes and roasting devices from which to hold or suspend the food or vessels around the fire. In the late 18th century the first cast iron ranges began to appear with a central open fire and an enclosed oven and boiler on either side. Although these open ranges became popular from 1800, some cooks still preferred roasting on an open fire and resisted change – or if there was the space had

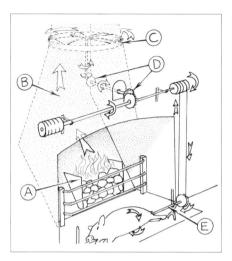

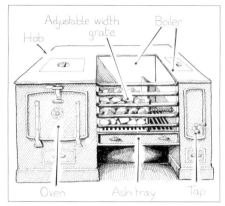

FIG 7.4: *A drawing of a kitchen grate with a smoke jack from a large Georgian house, showing the metal flanks (A) that could be adjusted to make the fire larger or smaller. The hot fumes from this rose up the flue (B) and turned the fan (C), which rotated the shafts (D) and via a pulley the spit (E) in front of the fire.*

FIG 7.5: *An early cast iron open range, which became available in the late 18th century, with an oven to the left and a boiler on the right of the grate. Unlike a modern cooker, which you simply switch on and is cleaned by self cleaning liners, the cast iron range was time consuming, complicated and dirty. Fires were kept lit continuously (helping to protect basement kitchens from damp), controlling the heat was notoriously tricky and took an experienced hand, and the range needed regular black leading.*

both. From the 1830s more economical ranges, where the central fire was enclosed on the top with a removable door in front, became popular.

A long table for the preparation of dishes would have stood in the middle of the kitchen. It was usually made of pine, scrubbed to a pale colour with the grain showing proud after years of sanding and washing. Slatted wooden boards might be positioned around the table for the cook and servants to stand on, while the floor beneath was solid, composed of stone flags or tiles. A dresser would have stood against a wall with open shelving above and below (sometimes enclosed underneath) for cooking utensils, pots and pans and some dinnerware.

SCULLERY OR BACK KITCHEN

The back kitchen, later more generally called a scullery (derived from the French word for 'dish', which in turn comes from the Latin word *scutella*, meaning 'salver', hence it was where the plates and dishes were washed up), was next door to the main kitchen (usually behind it in a terraced house). It was a versatile space, which was used for

FIG 7.6: *A portable roasting spit was an ingenious device to cook small joints. The open face was positioned in front of the fire and a clockwork mechanism at the top rotated the meat hanging from the chain, with the concave back helping to reflect the heat onto the joint.*

FIG 7.7: *The back kitchen or scullery was where the washing up of cooking implements and the laundry were done. In this example there is a shallow stone sink with a wooden bowl for washing, a hand pump raising water from a well below (or nearby), a copper in the corner, and a small fire on which irons could be heated.*

messy tasks like preparing meat and gutting fish, as well as being where the washing up and laundry were done (the largest houses might have had a separate laundry). The floor would be flagged, tiled or brick, usually with a slope or central drain to take away the water.

The room would have contained a sink, which was generally wide and flat (deeper ceramic types only became widely available in the 19th century) and made of stone or wood with a watertight lead sheet lining. Wooden tubs might have been set within the sink for washing up delicate items like china. Water was collected either from a well or rainwater butts, although sometimes a well was positioned beneath the floor with a hand pump above next to the sink for convenience. The water was generally heated up in a copper, especially from the late 18th century when soap, which required hot water for the best effect, became popular for laundry (previously lye had been used, a solution made from boiling and straining wood ash, which was used with cold water). The copper was a round metal tank set in a brick or stone frame (usually in a corner) with a fire below to heat the water for both washing up and laundry.

Washday was generally dreaded by the staff and, unlike today when you simply flick a switch, it was time consuming and hard work. There were tubs and boards for washing and scrubbing with lye or soap, and there might have been a mangle for wringing out large and heavy pieces. Drying racks were suspended from the ceiling on pulleys or positioned in front of a fire for smaller items. There might also

FIG 7.8: *A copper with a wooden lid covering the bowl in which the water was held and an opening below. This accessed the fire and had a gap underneath from which the ashes could be removed.*

have been a space out in the garden or yard for drying. Ironing was done with metal irons heated on the fire and pressed down on a table covered with a sheet.

FIG 7.9: COGGES MANOR FARM, WITNEY, OXFORDSHIRE: *A selection of laundry equipment in a shallow stone sink.*

CELLARS AND LARDERS

Storage of food was a problem in the days before refrigerators and modern methods of preservation. Cellars, larders and pantries had to be as cool as possible to maximise the shelf life. There might have been a single cellar in a basement or a series of them beneath a large house. They were used for storing wine and beer casks, dry goods and candles, and hanging meat and game, and would have had a low, vaulted ceiling, stone, tile or brick floors (often with drains to keep the damp down), usually no window and only limited ventilation to keep them cool.

Larders (from the Latin *lardum*, meaning 'bacon') or a pantry (from the Latin *panis*, meaning 'bread') were traditionally where the meat and bread were stored but the latter was more

FIG 7.10: *Larders were usually accessed directly from the kitchen and were used to store some meats, fish and dairy products. To keep the larder cool it was usually positioned on the north or east side with a small gauze opening and stone shelves within.*

flexible by this period and was often referred to as the dry larder; there may have been both in a large house. A general larder would suffice in a medium sized house and it would have had a solid floor, stone shelves at waist height to keep produce cool, wooden ones above and hooks for hanging meat. Again, like the cellars, it would only have had the smallest of openings to the outside and was preferably positioned to the cool north side of the house.

OTHER ROOMS

In the largest houses there would have been additional rooms for specific tasks, which increased in number in the Regency period. In most houses the servants would have eaten within the kitchen after the meals had been served but in the largest examples a separate hall was generally provided for them.

Beer was drunk at meal times, including breakfast, by most of the family as water quality was unreliable and the brewing process purified it. A brewhouse was often found at the rear of large houses, especially in the country.

The senior members of a large household would expect their own rooms. There would be a butler's pantry positioned near the rear and close to the dining room (the smooth running of which was his responsibility) and the wine cellar. He used it as an office, a safe place for keeping the best table linen, cutlery, crockery and glasses, a space for cleaning and polishing silver, and as a living room and bedroom. The housekeeper's room was often at the front of the basement where she could keep an eye on the comings and goings of the staff and store the bulk of the tableware.

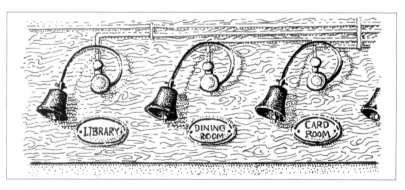

FIG 7.11: *In the Regency period the servants were summoned by bells, which were hung from a board and connected to pull cords in each room by fine wires running through pipes in the walls. The bells would often have a hanging piece attached (not shown) and this would continue to vibrate for some time so they could tell which one had rung if it was missed. Previously servants had to sit in the hall and wait to be summoned.*

CHAPTER 8

Yards and Gardens

FIG 8.1: *The rears of even spacious urban terrace houses were not a space for leisure. They were usually yards with service rooms and mews in the largest examples or small paved yards with a privy, coal and ash bins and a water butt, as in this example, at the back of a medium sized Georgian terrace.*

The area immediately outside the Georgian and Regency houses differed in many ways from those of today, not only in appearance but also because of attitudes towards it. Gardening was not the popular hobby now enjoyed by practically everyone, with every tiny space turned over to greenery and flowers – in fact it did not exist as a pastime at all. The upper and middle classes would never be seen getting their hands dirty and the working masses rarely had the space to do so and then only if the activity involved foodstuffs or livestock. It was not until the later Victorian period,

FIG 8.2: CAVENDISH SQUARE, LONDON: *The square was a later planned development (rather than houses being built around an existing open space, park or village green) provided by the builder as space for the tenants of the surrounding houses to meet respectable society and as a safe sanctuary for children to play under the guidance of a parent or nanny. It was usually gated and railed off to keep unwanted visitors out.*

gardens today, while the backs of most terraces in this period were dark, damp spaces for the services where the owner would rarely venture.

THE FRONTS

The front of most Georgian houses directly abutted the pavement outside, although some larger examples were set slightly back behind railings with steps leading up to the front door. Later in the period it became common for the façade to be positioned behind a railed off well called the 'area', which provided improved lighting into the basement and a discreet entrance down the steps for servants and deliveries. This also gave the owners increased privacy as it became fashionable for staff to be more out of sight of guests.

This later arrangement meant that the basement was often only partly underground, a half basement, which reduced excavation costs for the builder and the front door was now raised up a set of steps, making a more imposing entrance. However, in many cases, the spoil from the foundations was used to build up the street in front, providing a space under the pavement for cellars accessed from the area of each house. At least one of these would have housed coal, which delivery men would drop down a chute set in the pavement with a removable metal cover to close it off when not in use, still a common sight today along many such terraces.

Railings were a common sight in front of larger houses, usually to prevent people falling into the area but also as a decorative feature. Most from

when flushing toilets and earth closets were re-housed within a rear extension and drainage improved, that respectable people started to regard their garden as a place to cultivate plants and flowers.

There was also an emphasis on the front of the house, which was a public place to be looked upon by passers by and from which the householders could gaze at those outside. There was little of our current obsession for privacy as the house was very much a venue for respectable society. Pavements for promenading and enclosed squares of greenery in front of larger urban terraces were used as we might our rear

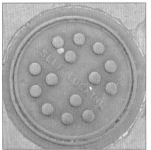 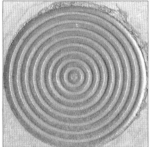 

FIG 8.3: *Circular metal covers set in the pavement can still be found above the old chutes down which coal was poured into the storage cellar below. This indicates that the road was built up from spoil dug out from the house foundations and a rise in height can sometimes be found where it meets older roads on the original ground level.*

this period were of simple designs with a single horizontal bar along the top and the bases of each vertical set into a raised sill or directly into the ground (later types or modern replacements usually have a horizontal bar top and bottom). With improved casting in the first decades of the 19th century more elaborate and delicate designs were available. In these days before street lighting (although some early gas lamps did appear towards the end of the Regency period) torches were used by footmen to light lanterns and were put out by conical snuffers, while lamps suspended in metal rings over the steps or at the side provided additional light (see Fig 4.35).

THE REARS

Most urban houses had little more than a paved or gravel yard at the rear. This walled space, sometimes backing onto a rear passageway, but other times accessed only through the house, was

FIG 8.4: BLACK COUNTRY MUSEUM, DUDLEY, WEST MIDLANDS: *The privy, bog house or jakes was typically a tall brick structure with a hole cut into a set of planks providing the seat above a cesspit or drains. Cesspits were filled with either earth or ash and were emptied out by nightsoil men a few times a year.*

FIG 8.5: *The mews, which ran along the rear road at the back of large houses, was used for storing the owner's carriage and horses, usually with a second storey above for the staff. Most examples today have become garages or have been sold off and converted into homes or flats. In other later examples (bottom right) service rooms like the kitchen were sited out here.*

essential for the storage of the basic services. Coal for the fires and ranges was kept here when there was not a suitable cellar elsewhere, and the ash, which the average house produced in vast quantities, was also stored in the yard. The privy, usually no more than a hole in planks of wood suspended above a cesspit or, in later properties, above drains leading off into a local watercourse, was also here although the owners of the house would use the closets or chamber pots indoors and the servants would carry them outside for emptying. As running water on tap was a rarity until the Regency period most houses had water butts collecting the rain via guttering, usually for washing rather than drinking, and if there was space there might also be room for drying laundry.

Larger urban houses, especially later in the period, would have many of the services housed out here in rear extensions or separate buildings. Kitchens, sculleries and, in the largest houses, a laundry or even brewhouse could be found where space permitted. It was also common on most big terraced houses to have a mews along the rear, backing onto a private road. These were the double garages of their day where horses and carriages could be stabled on the ground floor with room for the staff above. Most of these have been sold off and converted into flats or garages in the 20th century but, as such, have retained their overall structure, often with the cobbled back lane.

Although the rear of most houses was an odorous place, a few houses were fortunate enough to have space for a private garden especially early in the period before land prices shot up. The owner in this period, however, would only admire and use it for recreation and leave maintenance to a gardener. The largest detached or terraced houses could have had room for a walled garden with space to grow produce for use in the kitchen and at the rear for a conservatory or extension for an additional room. It was more likely that a small flat rectangular space would be provided with beds and gravel paths for the owners when the services could be housed in or around the house and there was good drainage for the privy. Later in the Regency period the square at the front, around which the terraces were arranged, provided a similar role.

FIG 8.6: *Gardens at the rear were not common but did exist in some of the largest houses, as in these examples restored from records and excavations at The Circus, Bath (left) and Pickford's House, Derby (right).*

SECTION III

QUICK
REFERENCE
GUIDE

D ating a house can be achieved visually and with documentation, the former giving only an approximate time-frame but quickly, the latter more time consuming but potentially more exact. In most cases it will only be through a combination of a number of datable features and a selection of facts from various documents that the approximate date of construction will be found. This task is trickier for Georgian housing when information and especially maps are harder to find and not always accurate, but easier for the later Regency buildings as there are generally more documents and records, and styles began to be less regionalised and easier to date.

Datestones: You may be fortunate enough simply to have a date emblazoned on the exterior of your house. It may appear in the form of a plaque, a keystone (the central segment of an arch or lintel over a door) or on the rainwater trap at the top of guttering. Be very wary, though, as this is often recording a later makeover and not the original date of the main structure. Georgians had the opposite attitude towards houses than we do today – then it was modern that should be celebrated and old that should be hidden! It was very common in this period for owners to give the façade a makeover in the latest style when they could not afford to rebuild the entire house. For instance, new cast iron guttering would proudly display the date so the whole property would appear more modern.

Visual Dating: The following time chart, which shows the style of external details that were popular in approximate time-frames, and the photographs in Chapter 4 will help you identify the time when your house was likely to have been built. Look at the pitch of the roof, the style of original windows and doors, the

FIG 9.1: DATESTONES: *Examples of dates that can be found on rainwater traps, plaques and keystones.*

bonding and uniformity of the brick, the position and prominence of the chimney, the presence or not of a rear extension and the form of details like sash windows and classical ornamentation. It is also important to look at and find out more about similar houses in your street or local area, especially if there are ones that are of a similar structure in your row but have retained datable original features. However, yet again, caution is needed as, firstly, houses were often built in small numbers of perhaps two or three; others in the same row could have been erected by different builders at an earlier or later date. Fashions also reached areas at different times and although it is assumed in the past that they originated in London and spread out across the country over the following decades, the improvements in transport and new architectural publications in the second half of the period meant that new ideas could travel quickly and to distant parts in a seemingly haphazard manner. For instance, a forward thinking aristocrat might bring the latest fashion in London to his remote country estate and use it upon houses in the estate village, long before the style came into general use in the neighbouring towns.

Documentary Evidence: Documentary evidence is usually essential for dating houses from this period with greater accuracy. There are a number of sources listed below, most of which are available from your local or county library, which are a good starting point. If these, however, prove fruitless the bibliography lists a number of books that will take your research further.

Maps: Local or county libraries usually store maps from this period, although before the 19th century there was no general mapping agency and it is only through luck that your area may have been surveyed for an enclosure act or sale of land. The first editions of the Ordnance Survey small-scale maps (1 inch to a mile) date from 1805–73 but could be inaccurate (republished by David and Charles). They are a quick and easy way to see when your house appears, but be careful when interpreting the date on the map as there were revisions to add new railways and roads and it is important to check any accompanying notes for the sheet you are using. They also are only telling you that it was there by the time of the survey and not when it was actually built.

Victoria County Histories: A detailed series of books, which after a century are still only half complete! If your town or village is covered it could save you digging through old documents to piece together the history of your parish and background to your house. They are packed with useful information and often tell you when an area or road was laid out (although the houses built along it may date from some time after).

Listing: All houses from this period should be listed, Grade II for the majority, Grade II* and Grade I for the most exceptional. Either the local library or council offices should have a record of this listing, often a survey done by county officials or architectural experts looking at the properties in question. This may be the easiest way to find an approximate date for your house but as internal inspection is not always possible there may be limits to their value.

'The Buildings of England' series: An indispensable series of books begun some forty to fifty years ago by the architectural expert Nicholas Pevsner (and revised with up-to-date notes by many others) that cover each county, commenting on and dating buildings of note in each town or village. The degree to which your area is covered may vary but if you are lucky many quite modest houses may be recorded and given approximate dates, while notable houses are studied more accurately.

Other sources: If you have access to your deeds they may simply answer the question; if not it might be possible to find out who was the landlord, often a company, university or landed estate, and their records, estate papers and building accounts can be useful. Local history books and groups are always a good source of information. Trade directories for the local area list addresses and can tell you when a house existed but are only generally available for the later part of this period. Also try tithe surveys (late 1830s) in the Public Record Office, plans for new roads and canals, fire insurance records, and local papers.

Above all with tracing the history of your house, where time permits, always work from the whole to the part. That is, look at the general history of your local area before getting bogged down with the tiniest details on the house itself.

STU'T | Queen Anne → | George I → | George II → | George III

1710 1720 1730 1740 1750 1760 1770

▲ South Sea Bubble ▲ Jacobite Rebellion ← Seven Years War → ▲ 1774 Building Act

BAROQUE ROCOCO ADAM

PALLADIAN

Bolection moulding

Gibbs surrounds

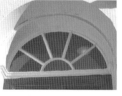

Simple fanlights

Double pile houses

Neo classic details

Exposed sash boxes

REGENCY   VICT

George III →| Prince Regent |← George IV →| William IV |← Q.Vic—

| 1780 | 1790 | 1800 | 1810 | 1820 | 1830 | 1840 |

American
Independence

French
Revolution

Napoleonic
Wars

Death of
George III

Great
Reform
Act

Battle of Trafalgar

Battle
of Waterloo

ADAM   GOTHICK

NEO CLASSICAL

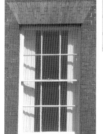

More elaborate
fanlights

Shallow pitch roofs

Sash boxes behind
brickwork

Bow windows   Gothick windows   Ironwork balconies

BIBLIOGRAPHY

The following books may also be useful for further information:

Social History

Hibbert, Christopher *The English: A Social History 1066–1945* (1994)
Iredale, David and Barrett, John *Discovering Local History* (1999)
Sheppard, Francis *London: A History* (1999)
Strong, Roy *The Story of Britain* (1996)
Strong, Roy *The Spirit of Britain* (2000)
Taylor, Christopher *Village and Farmstead* (1983)
Williams, E.N. *Life in Georgian England* (1967)

Architecture

Avery, Derek *Georgian and Regency Architecture* (2003)
Breckon, Bill and Parker, Jeffrey *Tracing the History of Houses* (2000)
Brunskill, R.W. *Brick Building in Britain* (1990)
Brunskill, R.W. *Houses and Cottages of Britain* (1997)
Curl, James Stevens *Classical Architecture* (2001)
Currer-Briggs, Noel *Debrett's Guide to Your House* (no longer in print)
Dowdy, Mac; Miller, Judith; and Austin, David *Be Your Own House Detective* (1997)
Fleming, John; Honour, Hugh; and Pevsner, Nikolaus *The Penguin Dictionary of Architecture and Landscape Architecture* (1998)
Iredale, David and Barrett, John *Discovering Your Old House* (1997)
Pevsner, Nikolaus *The Buildings of England* (various counties)
Watkin, David *English Architecture* (2001)

Period Details

Eveleigh, David J. *Firegrates and Kitchen Ranges* (2000)
Cranfield, Ingrid *Georgian House Style* (2001)
Hall, Linda *Down the Garden Path: Privies in and around Bristol and Bath* (2001)
Hall, Linda *Period House Fixtures and Fittings 1300-1900* (2005)
Jackson, Albert and Day, David *Period House: How to Repair, Restore and Care for Your Home* (2005)
Lawrence, Richard Russell and Chris, Teresa *The Period House: Style, Detail and Decoration 1774-1914* (1998)
Miller, Judith *Period Fireplaces* (1996)
Miller, Judith *Period Details Sourcebook* (1999)
Rivers, Tony; Cruickshank, Dan; Darley, Gillian; and Pawley, Martin *The Name of the Room* (1992)

There are numerous websites with information on Georgian houses and especially on the fixtures and fittings and where to find them. If you enter the items you are looking for along with 'Georgian' into your search engine you should find good examples often from antique dealers and reclamation outlets. The following sites are just the ones I am aware of that may be useful for general research:

en.wikipedia.org
www.georgiangroup.org.uk
www.bricksandbrass.co.uk
www.architecture.com
www.britishlistedbuildings.co.uk
www.buildingconservation.com/articles/articles.htm
www.britainexpress.com/architecture/georgian.htm

BACK TO BACKS, 50-54 Inge Street, Birmingham, B5 4TE, Tel: 0121 666 7671; www.nationaltrust.org.uk/birmingham-back-to-backs. A rare glimpse inside working class homes restored to show how they would appear in different periods.

COGGES MANOR FARM MUSEUM, Church Lane, Witney, Oxfordshire, OX28 3LA, Tel: 01993 772602; www.cogges.org.uk . A restored farmhouse with a good example of a working country kitchen.

THE DARBY HOUSES, Darby Road, Coalbrookdale, Telford, TF8 7EW, Tel: 01952 433424; www.ironbridge.org.uk/our-attractions/darby-houses. Two former homes of the Darby family, Ironbridge's famous Quaker iron masters.

FAIRFAX HOUSE, Castlegate, York, YO1 9RN, Tel: 01904 655543, www.fairfaxhouse.co.uk . An elegant Georgian town house by John Carr close to the Jorvik Viking Centre and York Castle Museum.

GEFFRYE MUSEUM, Kingsland Road, London, E2 8EA, Tel: 020 7739 9893; www.geffrye-museum.org.uk. The leading museum of the British home with reconstructed interiors from 1600 to the present day.

GEORGIAN HOUSE (NTS), 7 Charlotte Sq, Edinburgh, EH2 4DR, Tel: 0131 226 3318; www.nts.org.uk/Property/Georgian-House. A beautifully restored late 18th century town house, part of a square designed by Robert Adam.

GEORGIAN HOUSE, 7 Great George Street, Bristol, BS1 5RR, Tel: 0117 921 1362, www.bristolmuseums.org.uk/georgian-house-museum. Outstanding restoration of the late 18th century home of John Pinney, a Bristol based slave trader.

NO 1 THE ROYAL CRESCENT, Bath, Avon BA1 2LR, Tel: 01225 428126; www.no1royalcrescent.org.uk. A house in the famous Royal Crescent with rooms restored back to their late 18th century appearance.

PICKFORD'S HOUSE MUSEUM, 41 Friar Gate, Derby, DE1 1DA, Tel: 01332 715181, www.derbymuseums.org/pickfords-house. A wonderfully restored Georgian townhouse and garden displaying the skills of the local architect Joseph Pickford.

THE REGENCY TOWN HOUSE, 13 Brunswick Square, Hove, Sussex, BN3 1EH, Tel: 01273 206306; www.rth.org.uk. A fine Regency house with restored interiors and displays about the development of Brighton during this period.

VICTORIA AND ALBERT MUSEUM, Cromwell Road, London, SW7 2RL, Tel: 020 7942 2000, www.vam.ac.uk. The finest collection of artwork, period furniture and interior fittings.

GLOSSARY

ACANTHUS:	Mediterranean plant used in a stylised form for decoration, especially by Neo Classical architects.
AEDICULE:	The surrounding of a window or door by a raised moulding or pilasters with a form of pediment across the top. Common on classically styled houses from the 1830s.
ANTHEMION:	A decorative motif based upon a honeysuckle flower.
ARCHITRAVE:	The lowest section of the entablature. In this context it refers to the door surround.
AREA:	Common name for the open space in front of a large terraced house down which steps lead to the basement.
ASHLAR:	Smooth, squared stone masonry with fine joints.
ASTYLAR:	A façade with no vertical features such as columns.
BALUSTER:	Plain or decorated post supporting the stair rail.
BALUSTRADE:	A row of decorated uprights (balusters) with a rail along the top.
BARGEBOARD:	External vertical boards that protect the ends of the sloping roof on a gable – they were often decorated.
BAY WINDOW:	A window projecting from the façade of a house up a single, or number of, storeys but always resting on the ground.
BOLECTION MOULDING:	Used to cover joints between two surfaces of different levels. Popular in the late 17th and early 18th century around doors and fireplaces.
BONDING:	The way bricks are laid in a wall with the different patterns formed by alternative arrangements of headers (**the short ends**) and stretchers (**the long side**).
BOW WINDOW:	A vertical projection (bay) of semi-circular or segmental plan.
CANTED:	An angled structure usually referring to a bay window.
CAPITAL:	The decorated top of a Classical column.
CASEMENT:	A window that is hinged along the side.
CHIMNEYBREAST:	The main body of the chimney including the fireplace and flues.
CHIMNEYPIECE:	An internal fireplace surround.
COPING STONE:	A protective capping running along the top of a wall.
CORNICE:	The top section of the entablature, which in this context refers to the moulding that runs around the top of an external or internal wall.
COVING:	A large concave moulding that covers the joint between the top of a wall and the ceiling.
DADO:	The base of a classical column, which in this context refers to the bottom section of a wall between the skirting and dado or chair rail.
DENTILS:	A row of small, square, alternately projecting decorations used as part of cornices and other mouldings.
DORMER:	An upright window set in the angle of the roof and casting light into the attic rooms.

EAVES:	The section of the roof timbers under the tiles or slates where they either meet the wall (and a parapet continues above) or project over it (usually protected by a fascia board, which supports the guttering).
EGG AND DART:	A decorative row of truncated egg shapes with arrows between used as part of mouldings.
ENTABLATURE:	The horizontal lintel supported by columns in a classical temple.
ENTASIS:	The slight bulging of classical columns in the middle to counter an optical illusion that makes them appear concave to the naked eye.
FAÇADE:	The main vertical face of the house.
FANLIGHT:	The window above a door lighting the hall beyond. Named after the radiating bars in semi-circular Georgian and Regency versions.
FENESTRATION:	The arrangement of windows in the façade of a house.
FIELDED:	The raised central part of a panel.
FINIAL:	An ornamental piece on top of a railing or the end of the roof ridge.
FLUTING:	The vertical concave grooves running up a column or pilaster.
FRIEZE:	The middle section of the entablature, in this context referring to the section of the wall between the picture rail and cornice.
GABLE:	The pointed upper section of wall at the end of a pitched roof.
GLAZING BARS:	The internal divisions of a window, which support the panes.
GUILLOCHE:	A decorative pattern made from two twisted bands forming circles between.
HEARTH:	The stone or brick base of a fireplace.
HUSK:	A seedcase shape used in decoration.
JAMBS:	The sides of an opening for a door or window.
KEYSTONE:	The top stone in an arch, often projected as a feature.
LINTEL:	A flat beam fitted over a door or window to take the load of the wall above.
LOGGIA:	An open side to a building, usually in the form of a series of open arches or columns.
MOULDING:	A decorative strip of wood, stone or plaster.
MULLION:	A vertical member dividing a window.
NEWEL:	The principal vertical post in a set of stairs.
ORIEL:	A projecting window supported from the wall rather than the ground.
PARAPET:	The top section of wall, continuing above the sloping end of the roof.
PARGETING:	A raised pattern formed from plaster on an external wall (popular originally in the East of England).
PEDIMENT:	A low pitched triangular feature supported by columns or pilasters, above a classically styled door or window in this context.

PIANO NOBILE: The principal floor for receiving guests usually on the first floor of a Georgian and Regency House.

PILASTER: A flat classical column fixed to a wall or fireplace and projecting slightly from it.

PITCH: The angle by which a roof slopes. A plain sloping roof of two sides is called a pitched roof.

PLINTH: The projecting base around a building.

PORTICO: A structure forming a porch over a doorway, usually with a flat cover supported by columns.

PURLIN: The principal horizontal beams in a roof structure.

QUOIN: The corner stones at the junction of walls. Often raised above the surface, made from contrasting materials or finished differently from the rest of the wall for decorative effect.

REEDING: Three or more parallel beads running vertically or horizontally for decoration, mainly in Regency houses.

RENDER: A protective covering for a wall.

REVEAL: The sides (jambs) of a recessed window or door opening.

RUBBLE: An arrangement of irregular sized stones in a wall either with no pattern or laid in rough courses (layers).

RUSTICATION: The cutting of stone or moulding of stucco into blocks separated by deep incised lines and sometimes with a rough hewn finish. Often used to highlight the base of a classically styled house.

SASH WINDOW: A window that slides vertically (or horizontally on smaller 'Yorkshire sash' windows).

SKIRTING: The protective strip of wood at the base of a wall.

STRING: The side support panel for a stair.

STRING COURSE: A horizontal band running across a façade and usually projecting.

STUCCO: A plaster used to render, imitate stonework and form decorative features, especially on classically styled houses.

SWAG: A decorative festoon of cloth, flowers or fruit suspended to form a 'smile' shape.

TRACERY: The ribs that divide the top of a stone window and are formed into patterns.

TRANSOM: The horizontal bar in a window.

VAULT: An arched structure of brick or stone used to cover a room or commonly in Georgian houses to form the basement or cellars.

VERNACULAR: Buildings made from local materials in styles and construction methods passed down within a distinct area, as opposed to architect designed structures made from mass produced materials.

VOUSSOIR: The wedged shaped stones or bricks that make up an arch.

WAINSCOT: Timber lining of internal walls or panelling.

YORKSHIRE SASH WINDOW: A sash window that slides horizontally and therefore does not require pulleys and weights, hence making it cheaper and popular on the top floors of working class housing.

Index